Welcome to the third edition of the

Cheltenham Festival Stallion Guid

Introduction from the Author – James Iddiols

When it comes to the Cheltenham Festival, there is compelling evidence that a horse's breeding is a critical factor when it comes to picking winners. The progeny of some stallions perform creditably at the festival time and time again, whereas others consistently struggle. This Guide analyses each sire's festival record based upon the performance and results of that sire's offspring over the past ten festivals. The result is an analysis and commentary on 44 stallions upon which there is evidence of a statistical trend and where the progeny are likely to be represented at the 2017 Cheltenham Festival. Armed with the Guide's clear-sighted information and recommendations, punters have a new angle on which to make their betting selections and hopefully improve their chances of beating the bookmakers.

My aim is not only to provide an analysis on each stallion that is easy to follow and insightful for betting purposes, but I also hope to successfully re-ignite fond memories for Cheltenham Festival devotees by highlighting previous races and runners together with some fascinating observations and thought-provoking festival trivia.

Looking back at the 2016 Cheltenham Festival, it was a rather unusual discovery to find that in the thick of the action of 28 glorious races, there was just one winner with a starting price of greater than 16/1. Typically at a festival, one can expect to see four or more big priced winners. Moreover, the number of winning favourites that we are used to seeing at the festival meeting usually ranges between 6 and 9, and yet last year, there were eleven winning favourites. Is this the start of a new trend? I don't believe so, but it certainly wasn't a good year for the bookmakers.

With regard to the analysis and advice provided within the Stallion Guide last year, for the most part, the recommendations were accurate. The jewel in the crown was highlighting how **Westerner**'s offspring have a knack of coming up with big priced festival winners and then witnessing last year's two biggest priced festival winners of 28/1 and 16/1 being **Westerner** bred! In addition, the results from last year supported my positive views about runners sired by **Astarabad, Gold Well, Midnight Legend, Milan, Robin Des Champs** and **Voix Du Nord**, as well as my negative opinion about the chances of those entries sired by **Beneficial, Definite Article** and **Flemensfirth**. That said, *Ivanovich Gorbatov* ruined my prediction that **Montjeu**'s brood would never again win at the festival and I was certainly surprised by three winners at the meeting for **Kayf Tara**'s progeny.

In this year's Guide, I have featured ten "new entries", generally younger stallions whose offspring have started to provide some early positive or negative festival trends. The sires making their debut appearance in the Cheltenham Festival Stallion Guide are **Al Namix, Assessor, Authorized, Ballingarry, Cape Cross, Fragrant Mix, High Chaparral, Kapgarde, Saddler Maker** and **Shirocco**. I have also dropped seven stallions from the Guide, either because the sire is not producing the quality of offspring rated high enough to get a run at the festival or simply due to the fact that the stallion's progeny are now too old to race. The seven who have appeared in previous Stallion Guides, but are not featured in 2017 are **Accordion, Alderbrook, Dansili, Exit To Nowhere, Indian Danehill, King's Best** and **Witness Box**.

After I had just completed last year's Guide, a friend of mine suggested that for 2017, I may wish to include an index table of the stallions and their progeny. I have taken his advice, and at the back of the Guide, there is a table of the stallions featured in the Guide along with a list of their offspring that, as of January 2017, were showing an official rating of 130 or greater.

Readers may be interested to know that the 44 stallions listed in this 2017 Cheltenham Festival Stallion Guide produced 19 of last year's 28 winners. 492 horses took part in the 2016 Cheltenham Festival, of which 54%, or 264 runners, were sired by stallions featured in this year's Guide. For the record, a total of 727 stallions have been responsible for the 4,775 entries to have run at the festival in the past decade, and of those, 16% have had ten or more festival runners.

I hope you enjoy reading this year's Stallion Guide and if you have any views or comments, please feel free to contact me on Twitter @festivalsires. I wish you all an enjoyable and rewarding 2016 Cheltenham Festival.

Finally, I would like to say a very big thank you to my wife, Katherine, for her unwavering support and patience in allowing me the space and time required to write this Guide.

James Iddiols @festivalsires

Highlights from the 2016 Cheltenham Festival Stallion Guide

Quotes from the 2016 Cheltenham Festival Stallion Guide	What happened at the festival?
"The recommendation to punters is to draw a line through any **Definite Article** bred entries who line up at the 2016 Cheltenham Festival."	The performances from the three runners sired by **Definite Article** read as Fell, Pulled Up, 20th
"The *Ultima Handicap Chase*, a Grade 3 chase run over a distance of 3m½f, has been a successful event over the past two years for **Gold Well**'s supporters."	In the 2016 *Ultima Handicap Chase*, the **Gold Well** sired, ***Holywell***, finished second at odds of 8/1.
"The finishing positions from **Midnight Legend**'s stock reveal that 17 of the 35 runs have resulted in a top six finish, and of those 17 runs, eight of the horses had a starting price of 25/1 or greater."	Of the 10 **Midnight Legend** sired runners, 5 achieved a top six finish of which four were priced up at 25/1 or greater.
"Over the past three Cheltenham Festivals, punters have received a return for close to one in every three runs from **Milan**'s progeny. That's good enough for me."	**Milan**'s offspring attained two victories and a 3rd place dividend from nine entries.
"**Robin Des Champs** is just 19 years old, and on the basis that he remains alive and well, I'm convinced that in the years to come, we will witness many more Cheltenham Festival victories from the progeny of this record breaking sire."	Two wins from the progeny. ***Vautour*** (*Ryanair Chase*) and ***Un Temps Pour Tout*** (*Ultima Handicap Chase*).
"With two victories and three place dividends from just 18 festival runs, the future looks bright for this young 17 year old stallion. And supporters of **Westerner**'s offspring have been rewarded with some big price festival successes."	The two biggest priced winners at the 2016 Cheltenham Festival were both sired by **Westerner**. ***Empire Of Dirt*** (16/1 winner of the *Brown Advisory & Merriebelle Stable Plate*) and ***Solar Impulse*** (28/1 winner of the *Johnny Henderson Grand Annual Chase Challenge Cup*).

Contents

Introduction 1
Highlights from the 2016 Cheltenham Festival Stallion Guide.. 3

Stallions

Al Namix.. 5
Alflora 7
Assessor 9
Astarabad.. 11
Authorized 13
Ballingarry 15
Beneficial 17
Cape Cross 20
Definite Article 22
Dom Alco 23
Dr Massini 25
Flemensfirth.. 27
Fragrant Mix.. 29
Galileo 31
Germany.. 33
Gold Well 35
Hernando 37
Heron Island.. 38
High Chaparral 40
Kalanisi 42
Kapgarde 44
Karinga Bay.. 46
Kayf Tara 48
King's Theatre... 51
Midnight Legend 57
Milan 59
Montjeu 62
Old Vic 64
Oscar 67
Poliglote 71
Presenting 73
Robin Des Champs 76
Saddler Maker 78
Saint Des Saints 80
Shantou 82
Shirocco 84
Sinndar.. 86
Sir Harry Lewis 88
Stowaway 90
Turgeon 92
Turtle Island 94
Voix Du Nord 96
Westerner 99
Winged Love 101

Index Table by Stallion 103

Al Namix (FR)

Al Namix was not featured in the 2016 Cheltenham Festival Stallion Guide.

Al Namix (20-y-o)							
Race Format	_Miles_	_Won_	_Placed_	_Unplaced_	_Total_	_Win %_	_Place %_
Hurdles	About 2m	0	1	6	7	0%	14%
	About 2m 4f	0	0	4	4	0%	0%
	About 3m	0	1	1	2	0%	50%
Chases	About 2m	0	0	1	1	0%	0%
	About 2m 4f	0	0	1	1	0%	0%
	About 3m	0	0	1	1	0%	0%
	About 4m	0	0	1	1	0%	0%
Bumper	About 2m	0	0	0	0	-	-
Total		**0**	**2**	**15**	**17**	**0%**	**12%**

It is early days with **Al Namix**. There have only been 17 races at Cheltenham Festivals where the progeny have been represented, and so far we are still awaiting the first **Al Namix** bred festival winner. The closest that the offspring have come to recording a first festival win, has come from probably the two most recognised names of **Al Namix**'s stock, these being *Grandouet* and *Saphir Du Rheu.*

Grandouet's first run at a Cheltenham Festival occurred in the 2011 *JCB Triumph Hurdle*, and the *Nicky Henderson* trained 13/2 shot ran very respectably to finish 3rd in the race and a neck ahead of the 4/1 favourite, *Sam Winner*. *Grandouet* ran twice more at festival meetings, falling when travelling comfortably 4 out in the 2013 *Stan James Champion Hurdle Challenge Trophy* and then registering a 6th placing in the 2014 *Racing Post Arkle Challenge Trophy Chase*. *Saphir Du Rheu* has also participated at three Cheltenham Festivals. Being one of the 6/1 joint favourites in the 2013 *Fred Winter Juvenile Handicap Hurdle*, he ran very disappointingly to finish 20th of 24 runners. Having missed the 2014 Cheltenham Festival, he returned two years later, this time as the outright 5/1 favourite, in the 2015 *Ladbrokes World Hurdle*. Although it was a much better performance from *Saphir Du Rheu*, he came up against a rival who was just too good on the day in the shape of 14/1 shot, *Cole Harden*, who made all and stayed on strongly at the finish to win by 3¼ lengths. *Saphir Du Rheu* returned to Cheltenham, along with three other **Al Namix** sired runners, at last year's meeting. Once again, he took his chance in the *World Hurdle*, this time sponsored by *Ryanair*, but he was nowhere near good enough to match his effort of the preceding year, and was a well beaten 6th in a race that was won by the incredibly impressive *Thistlecrack*.

In looking at the 17 festival performances to date, my early impression is that **Al Namix**'s progeny have been a few notches below the level required to win races at the Cheltenham Festival. My rationale is based upon a 5th or 6th finishing position in five of the offspring's 17 festival races. My opinion may be different if the five runners were all big price outsiders, but this is not the case. In fact, of the 17 festival appearances from **Al Namix**'s stock, eight of the runners lined up with odds of less than 10/1, including three favourites.

In summary, the progeny of **Al Namix** have so far flattered to deceive. And until the offspring start to deliver festival performances more in keeping with what the market would have us believe, then I will not be placing any wagers on **Al Namix** bred entries at the 2017 Cheltenham Festival.

Alflora (IRE)

Quote from the 2016 Cheltenham Festival Stallion Guide - "With just one victory and four placed efforts in the past decade, backing **Alflora**'s progeny is not a strategy that particularly appeals, even though the offspring's entries often provide supporters with a reasonable run for their money."

Alflora (28-y-o)							
Race Format	Miles	Won	Placed	Unplaced	Total	Win %	Place %
	About 2m	0	1	3	4	0%	25%
Hurdles	About 2m 4f	0	0	10	10	0%	0%
	About 3m	0	0	3	3	0%	0%
	About 2m	0	0	4	4	0%	0%
Chases	About 2m 4f	1	2	3	6	17%	50%
	About 3m	0	1	8	9	0%	11%
	About 4m	0	0	2	2	0%	0%
Bumper	About 2m	0	0	2	2	0%	0%
Total		**1**	**4**	**35**	**40**	**3%**	**13%**

Darna was the sole **Alflora** bred horse to race at the 2016 Cheltenham Festival. The *Kim Bailey* trained 25/1 shot, lined up for the second time in the *Brown Advisory & Merriebelle Stable Plate*, attempting to follow up his success of the previous season. In winning the 2015 renewal, he became the very first of **Alflora**'s progeny to record a Cheltenham Festival victory, a feat that was beyond the 53 **Alflora** sired runners who had tried previously. The outcome of the 2016 race was in stark contrast to the celebrations of the previous year, as *Darna* fell heavily at the 8th fence.

Before *Darna*'s 2015 victory, the four horses that had come closest to breaking the duck in the past decade were all placed in novice events at the festival. *Amaretto Rose* started as the 2/1 Favourite in the 2007 festival opener, the *Anglo Irish Bank Supreme Novices' Hurdle*, but could only manage third. The only other **Alflora** sired runner to start as a favourite at a Cheltenham Festival also managed to achieve a placed position, when *Wishfull Thinking* finished runner-up to *Noble Prince* in the 2011 *Jewson Novices' Chase (registered as the Golden Miller Novices' Chase)*. The other two runners in the past decade who have achieved a placed position were *Wayward Prince* (15/2) who finished third and less than a length behind *Bostons Angel* in the 2011 *RSA Chase*, and *Isn't That Lucky* who was runner-up, at odds of 11/1, in the 2009 *Jewson Novices' Handicap Chase* (same sponsor but a different race to the aforementioned *Golden Miller Novices' Chase*).

At the festival, the best performances from **Alflora**'s stock are over fences. In the past decade, the offspring have tackled the bigger obstacles on 21 occasions, with eleven of those runs resulting in a top six finish. Due to *Darna*'s sole victory coming at the rewarding odds of 33/1, anyone who had backed all of **Alflora**'s offspring in chase events since 2007, would now be better off by £9.20 to a £1.00 each way stake. Despite this profit, (which let's face it, is the result of a 33/1 winner), supporting **Alflora**'s stock over fences is not for me and would be hugely frustrating due to the tendency for the progeny to miss out on paid places. Seven of those eleven top six chase finishes resulted in a zero return for punters who had backed them.

If I am not willing to support **Alflora** bred horses in chase events, I am certainly not going anywhere near the offspring when it comes to hurdles. In 17 hurdle races within the past 10 years, only the aforementioned mare, **Amaretto Rose**, has managed a placing. And the progeny have only hit a top six placing twice more over the same period, both of which were courtesy of **Alasi**, another mare, who finished fourth in the *David Nicholson Mares' Hurdle* in 2011 and 2012.

There are unlikely to be many **Alflora** sired entries at the 2017 Cheltenham Festival and I, for one, won't waste my time looking for them.

Assessor (IRE)

Assessor was not featured in the 2016 Cheltenham Festival Stallion Guide.

Race Format	Miles	Won	Placed	Unplaced	Total	Win %	Place %
Assessor (Died as a 23-y-o in 2012)							
Hurdles	About 2m	0	1	1	2	0%	50%
	About 2m 4f	0	1	0	1	0%	100%
	About 3m	0	0	4	4	-	-
Chases	About 2m	1	0	1	2	50%	50%
	About 2m 4f	0	0	0	0	-	-
	About 3m	0	1	1	2	0%	50%
	About 4m	0	0	0	0	-	-
Bumper	About 2m	0	0	0	0	-	-
Total		**1**	**3**	**7**	**11**	**9%**	**36%**

The very first of **Assessor's** offspring to appear at a Cheltenham Festival was some racehorse, although very few would have seen it coming based on his festival debut run in 2005 when finishing 15th in the 2m½f *Letheby & Christopher Supreme Novices' Hurdle*. Later that year, *My Way De Solzen* was campaigned over longer distances, and having finished runner-up in a three mile handicap hurdle race at Haydock, trainer *Alan King* entered the five year old gelding for the Grade 1 *Totesport Long Walk Hurdle* at Chepstow on 27th December 2005, which he won comfortably at odds of 12/1. Following an odds-on victory in a 2m3f prep race at *Fontwell* in mid-February, *My Way De Solzen* then took on the best three mile hurdlers at Cheltenham in the *Ladbrokes World Hurdle*. It was a tough race, but jockey *Robert Thornton* just managed to beat the challenge of *Golden Cross* by a head, and *My Way De Solzen* won the big prize at odds of 8/1. After two more runs in three mile hurdle races, *Alan King* then tried *My Way De Solzen* over one mile less and over fences, and the horse must have been incredibly versatile because the strategy worked! Following four appearances in small field novice chases, at the 2007 Cheltenham Festival, *My Way De Solzen* had the pace to win the *Irish Independent Arkle Challenge Trophy Chase*, over a distance of two miles. It was the 17th race for *My Way De Solzen* since he had been with *Alan King*, and jockey *Robert Thornton* had ridden the horse to victory on 10 occasions. After the 2007 *Arkle*, *My Way De Solzen* went off the boil and failed to win again for *Messrs King* and *Thornton*, his next victory being three years later when he made his debut for trainer, *Gabe Mahon*, in a Point-to-Point event at *Upton-on-Severn*, winning the contest at odds of 3/1.

Taking into account the two pre-2007 *My Way De Solzen* festival appearances, there have been a total of only 13 festival runners where **Assessor** is named as the sire. Those 13 runs have been made by just five of **Assessor's** progeny, of which only one has failed to achieve a top five placing. Frankly, considering **Richmond** was a 150/1 outsider, it would have been a major surprise if the *P P C Turner* trained gelding had fared significantly better than his 16th place finish in last year's *St. James's Place Foxhunter Chase Challenge Cup*. Like **Richmond**, two more of **Assessor's** offspring have visited the Cheltenham Festival just once, of which one managed to reward punters with a place dividend. In the 2016 *Fred Winter Juvenile Handicap Hurdle*, finishing in 3rd and less than a length off the winner, was the 16/1 chance, **Coo Star Sivola**, trained by *Nick Williams* and ridden by his step-daughter, *Lizzie Kelly*. On Boxing Day 2015, less than three months earlier, *Lizzie Kelly* had made history by becoming the first woman jump jockey to win a Grade One race when *Tea For Two* landed the *Kauto*

Star Novices' Chase at *Kempton*. *Kelly* is no stranger to making headlines, especially on New Year's Day. She landed the first UK jumps race of the year on 1ˢᵗ January 2014 when *Aubusson* won the *Neptune Investment Management Novices' Hurdle* at Cheltenham's New Year's Day meeting. And she repeated the trick by winning the first UK National Hunt race of this year also, when in the 2017 renewal of the same race, she rode the previously highlighted *Coo Star Sivola* to victory, the horse that provided her with her 3ʳᵈ place in the *Fred Winter*.

The other **Assessor** bred horse that has appeared at Cheltenham just once is *Turn Over Sivola*, who at odds of 33/1, just missed out on a place dividend by less than a length when finishing fifth in the 2015 *A.P. McCoy Grand Annual Chase Challenge Cup*. The horse in front of him to finish 4ᵗʰ was *Ned Buntline*. Of more significance was the fact that the person riding the 4ᵗʰ horse home was the 2010 BBC Sports Personality of the Year, who having been knighted in January 2016, is now *Sir Anthony Peter McCoy OBE*, although he will always be referred to, by so many fans as simply "A P". The 4ᵗʰ place finish on *Ned Buntline* was *Tony McCoy*'s last Cheltenham Festival ride.

With **Richmond**, *Coo Star Sivola* and *Turn Over Sivola* having had one festival appearance apiece, the mathematicians amongst us will no doubt have calculated that the two remaining festival representatives of the offspring must be responsible for the other 10 contests in which **Assessor's** progeny have participated. *My Way De Solzen* has raced at the Cheltenham Festival on four occasions and is the only one of **Assessor's** stock to have tasted victory. I have already highlighted his two wins, preceded by his festival debut and 15ᵗʰ placing in the 2005 *Supreme Hurdle*. His last Cheltenham Festival appearance was in 2008 when he finished 5ᵗʰ in the *Ladbrokes World Hurdle*. *Reve De Sivola* is a name that may be recognised by many Cheltenham Festival devotees as a result of the *Nick Williams* trained stalwart being present at the National Hunt showpiece meeting on a prodigious six occasions between 2009 and 2015. In those six appearances, he finished in the first six on four occasions, securing a place dividend twice. Having finished 6ᵗʰ as a 4 year old in the 2009 *JCB Triumph Hurdle*, he managed to secure place dividends in the next two seasons, the first of which occurred over hurdles when he finished behind *Peddlers Cross* to take 2ⁿᵈ in the 2010 *Neptune Investment Management Novices' Hurdle* at odds of 15/2. In 2011, he tackled Cheltenham's larger obstacles over three miles in the *Stewart Family Spinal Research Handicap Chase*, and although well beaten, jockey *Daryl Jacob* managed to reward supporters by riding the 9/1 chance into 3ʳᵈ place. Having missed the 2012 festival due to injury, *Reve De Sivola* returned to Cheltenham in the 2013 *Ladbrokes World Hurdle*, finishing 4ᵗʰ and a head behind *Smad Place*, who overtook him for 3ʳᵈ spot in the dying strides. He took part in the *World Hurdle* for the following two seasons, but his starting prices of 33/1 and 20/1 accurately reflected his chances and he finished down the field on both occasions.

Summing up the festival appearances of **Assessor's** stock, consider these facts: (1) **Assessor's** progeny have registered 2 wins and 3 places from a total of 13 festival runs, providing an impressive win and place strike rate of 38%; (2) A top five finish has been the outcome on 7 of the 8 occasions in which the **Assessor** sired entry was racing at an SP of less than 20/1; (3) In the five races in which the **Assessor** bred runner was racing at odds of 20/1 or greater, two of the five runs resulted in a 5ᵗʰ and 6ᵗʰ placing; (4) Ignoring last year's run from the 150/1 outsider, **Richmond**, the other four of **Assessor's** offspring to appear at a Cheltenham Festival have all managed to secure a top five finish.

Assessor sired entries at the 2017 Cheltenham Festival will be few and far between, but for those that do turn up, the smart decision is to back them.

Astarabad (USA)

Quote from the 2016 Cheltenham Festival Stallion Guide - "I am still very interested in supporting **Astarabad** bred runners and a better than 1 in 4 chance of acquiring a return on my wagers when backing the progeny at the Cheltenham Festival is good enough for me."

Astarabad (Died as a 22-y-o in 2016)

Race Format	Miles	Won	Placed	Unplaced	Total	Win %	Place %
	About 2m	1	3	4	8	13%	50%
Hurdles	About 2m 4f	1	0	6	7	14%	14%
	About 3m	0	0	3	3	0%	0%
	About 2m	0	0	0	0	-	-
	About 2m 4f	0	0	2	2	0%	0%
Chases	About 3m	0	0	0	0	-	-
	About 4m	0	0	0	0	-	-
Bumper	About 2m	1	0	0	1	100%	100%
Total		**3**	**3**	**15**	**21**	**14%**	**29%**

In last year's Stallion Guide, I highlighted the fact that **Astarabad**'s progeny are providing punters with a return for one in every four festival races, and so it proved at the 2016 Cheltenham Festival, where a place dividend was secured from the offspring's three entries. The placing was courtesy of the mare, *Missy Tata*, ridden by *Bryan Cooper* and trained by *Gordon Elliott*, who managed to take the fourth place dividend in the *Fred Winter Juvenile Handicap Hurdle*, at odds of 10/1. This handicap race, run over a distance of 2m½f, and open to four year old novice hurdlers has so far been a happy hunting ground for **Astarabad** sired runners. In four races in the event, the progeny have a 100% record of providing punters with a return. In the 2007 renewal of the race, we witnessed the first ever **Astarabad** sired horses to run at a Cheltenham Festival, when *Gaspara* and *Laustra Bad*, both trained by *David Pipe*, lined up in the race at odds of 9/2 and 16/1 respectively. Ridden by 5lb claimer, *Andrew Glassonbury*, *Gaspara* made all to win the race and pick up a £75,000 bonus, having landed the *Sunderlands Imperial Cup Handicap Hurdle* at Sandown just three days earlier. The joint favourite was unchallenged and crossed the line 5 lengths clear of *Altilhar*, who took second in the dying strides to finish a neck ahead of *Laustra Bad*, ridden by *Tom Scudamore*. The following year, in the 2008 *Fred Winter Juvenile Novices' Handicap Hurdle*, **Astarabad** sired *Grand Schlem*, trained by French trainer, *Francois Doumen*, attempted to follow up *Gaspara*'s success in the contest. Despite being up with the leaders and well in touch, *Grand Schlem* was a little one paced and eventually finished in third, at odds of 12/1. *Missy Tata*'s 4th in the race last year for **Astarabad**'s offspring means that all three of the offspring's place positions, as shown in the above table, have been achieved in the *Fred Winter*.

Ten **Astarabad** sired racehorses have experienced the Cheltenham Festival, and six of them have managed to reward supporters with a victory or a place, which is some accomplishment. Of those ten festival contestants, five of them have raced at more than one meeting, including all three winners. After her success in the 2007 *Fred Winter*, *Gaspara* just missed out on a place the following season when finishing 4th in the 2008 *David Nicholson Mares' Hurdle*. Settling for 5th in the same mares' race the following season, *Gaspara* then raced again just three days later in the 2009 *Martin Pipe Conditional Jockeys' Handicap Hurdle*, where she was unseated at the second flight.

The other two **Astarabad** bred winners had a similar profile to *Gaspara* in that, having won on their Cheltenham Festival debuts, they were unable to follow up with a win or place in any future festival events. In 2014, at odds of 14/1, jockey *Nico de Boinville* secured his first ever festival victory when riding **Whisper** to victory in the *Coral Cup*. It was an unforgettable day for the jockey as he won the race by a short head from *Get Me Out Of Here*, ridden by champion jockey, *A P McCoy*. In 2015, trainer *Nicky Henderson* entered **Whisper** in the *Ladbrokes World Hurdle*, where *Barry Geraghty* managed to have the horse disputing 2nd before the last, until weakening up the Cheltenham hill to eventually finish 5th. In the 2016 *Ryanair World Hurdle*, *Nico de Boinville*, was back in the saddle, but could do no better than *Mr Geraghty* the year before, as *Whisper* finished a well beaten 8th.

The other festival victor was the *Philip Hobbs* trained **Cheltenian**, who won the 2011 *Weatherbys Champion Bumper* at odds of 14/1. After missing the 2012 festival due to a tendon injury, **Cheltenian** returned to Cheltenham to compete in 2m hurdle events in successive years between 2013 and 2016. All four of these runs, however, were disappointing with 8th being the highest position attained, meaning that **Cheltenian** is the sole culprit for all four unplaced efforts showing in the above table's 2m hurdle category. After his 15th placing in the 2016 *Vincent O'Brien County Handicap Hurdle*, **Cheltenian** then headed up to *Haydock* for what was to be his last ever appearance on a racecourse. Sadly, on 7th May 2016, in the Grade 3 *Swinton Hurdle*, **Cheltenian** was quickly pulled up after suffering a fatal injury.

In general, **Astarabad**'s offspring perform well at Cheltenham Festivals and if one had backed the progeny in all 21 appearances to date, it would have resulted in a profit of £16.43 to a £1.00 each way stake. Digging deeper into the results and performances reveal some other intriguing observations;

1. From a total of just 10 **Astarabad** bred racehorses to have experienced the Cheltenham Festival (making up the 21 runs in total), six of them rewarded supporters with a victory or a place on their festival debut.
2. And, if at first, you don't succeed, then in the case of **Astarabad**'s stock, give up. To date, five debutants (3 winners, 1 third and 1 unplaced), have attempted to win or place in festival races after their first festival experience, but with eleven follow-up runs between them, all have failed.
3. The four **Astarabad** sired 4 year olds to have run at the festival, were all entered in the *Fred Winter Juvenile Novices' Handicap Hurdle* and all four secured at least a place

Being cognizant of these considerations above, punters should be very interested in all **Astarabad** sired entries who are making their Cheltenham Festival debuts, and especially any four year olds that are entered in the *Fred Winter Juvenile Novices' Handicap Hurdle*. Also, on the basis that **Astarabad**'s offspring don't perform in subsequent festivals as well as they do on their debuts, it would appear that, should they run at Cheltenham this spring, then any bets on *Jolly's Cracked It*, **Missy Tata** or **Whisper**, will be money down the drain.

Authorized (IRE)

Authorized was not featured in the 2016 Cheltenham Festival Stallion Guide.

Race Format	Miles	Won	Placed	Unplaced	Total	Win %	Place %
	Authorized (13-y-o)						
Hurdles	About 2m	1	2	7	10	10%	30%
	About 2m 4f	0	1	1	2	0%	50%
	About 3m	0	0	1	1	0%	0%
Chases	About 2m	0	0	0	0	-	-
	About 2m 4f	0	0	0	0	-	-
	About 3m	0	0	0	0	-	-
	About 4m	0	0	0	0	-	-
Bumper	About 2m	0	0	1	1	0%	0%
Total		**1**	**3**	**10**	**14**	**7%**	**29%**

With five runners at last year's meeting, **Authorized's** offspring have now accumulated 14 festival appearances in total, providing just enough information on which to prepare an initial analysis and commentary. Based on the 14 runs from the progeny to date, there is a pattern showing that the more fancied of **Authorized's** stock are performing well at Cheltenham Festivals, whilst the outsiders are finishing well down the field in their races and performing to market expectations. As a guideline, the cut-off point for whether an **Authorized** bred festival runner is worth supporting or not, is a starting price of 16/1.

There have been six races in which horses sired by **Authorized** have lined up at a Cheltenham Festival with odds of 14/1 or shorter, and on five occasions a top six finish has been recorded, including two 3rd place finishes and one winner. Those 3rd placings were achieved by *Nichols Canyon*, who has finished in the first three positions in 14 of his 15 hurdle races, the exception being when he unseated jockey *Ruby Walsh* in the *Paddy Power Future Champions Novice Hurdle* at *Leopardstown* in December 2014. The bay gelding was the 7/2 favourite on his first Cheltenham Festival appearance in the 2015 *Neptune Investment Management Novices' Hurdle*, when he clinched 3rd spot, a neck in front of the staying on, *Vyta Du Roc*. Last season, **Nichols Canyon** was one of three *Willie Mullins* representatives for the 2016 *Stan James Champion Hurdle Challenge Trophy*, and the 15/2 chance had to settle for 3rd place for the second time at a festival, being no match for the stable's first string and favourite for the race, *Annie Power*, who made all and won easily.

Authorized's progeny have been represented in the *JCB Triumph Hurdle* for three successive years, and the first of those three appearances resulted in the sole festival winner so far for the offspring. **Tiger Roll**, at odds of 10/1, kicked off a very special day for the horse's owners, *Gigginstown House Stud*, who racked up an incredible 82,653/1 four timer on Friday 14th March 2014, having had the fortune of seeing three more of their horses claim victory out of the six races that followed. In the 2015 running of the *JCB Triumph Hurdle*, **Beltor** (7/1), was attempting to make it a second successive victory for **Authorized's** progeny in the race, but as it turned out, he was a well beaten sixth. Although disappointing, **Beltor** did at least hit a top six finish, unlike **Zubayr** who was **Authorized's** representative in last year's renewal of the *Triumph*, and who ran very disappointingly to finish 13th of 15 runners. The result means that the *Paul Nicholls* trained, **Zubayr**, is the only one of

Authorized's offspring to have made a festival appearance at odds shorter than 16/1 and not to have secured a top six finish.

The fifth top six finish for **Authorized**'s stock that were towards the front of the betting market, happened in the 2013 *Fred Winter Juvenile Handicap Hurdle*, a race in which the progeny had three entries. The shortest price of those three runners, *Totalize*, from *Brian Ellison*'s stable in North Yorkshire, just missed out on the places when finishing 5th at odds of 14/1. The other two **Authorized** bred runners in the race, *Zamdy Man* and *Fatcatinthehat*, both at 20/1, finished 12th and 18th respectively, down the field performances that are in accordance with the finishing positions of all but one of the offspring's festival outsiders. For the record, seven of the eight **Authorized** sired runners who lined up at odds of 16/1 or bigger, ended up with finishing positions between 12th and 18th. The one exception happened at last year's festival, when the *Philip Hobbs* trained 33/1 shot, *Sternrubin*, well and truly broke the trend for **Authorized** bred outsiders, when taking 3rd place in the 2016 *Vincent O'Brien County Handicap Hurdle*.

In conclusion, from a pure financial perspective, if one had backed all fourteen **Authorized** bred festival runners to date, it would have resulted in a small loss of just 55p. Nevertheless, having achieved a victory and three places already, my view is that **Authorized**'s offspring have made a reasonable fist of it at Cheltenham Festivals so far, and although the data is still rather limited, for punters who fancy a wager on the progeny, I would advise that they should probably limit themselves to those priced at 14/1 or shorter.

Ballingarry (IRE)

Ballingarry was not featured in the 2016 Cheltenham Festival Stallion Guide.

Ballingarry (18-y-o)							
Race Format	*Miles*	*Won*	*Placed*	*Unplaced*	*Total*	*Win %*	*Place %*
	About 2m	1	1	0	2	50%	100%
Hurdles	About 2m 4f	0	0	5	5	0%	0%
	About 3m	0	0	1	1	0%	0%
	About 2m	0	0	0	0	-	-
Chases	About 2m 4f	0	1	1	2	0%	50%
	About 3m	0	0	2	2	0%	0%
	About 4m	0	0	0	0	-	-
Bumper	About 2m	0	0	0	0	-	-
Total		**1**	**2**	**9**	**12**	**8%**	**25%**

Preceding the 2016 Cheltenham Festival, **Ballingarry**'s progeny had registered a runner-up spot from eight festival appearances. The 2nd place was achieved by *Katgary*, who was always being held, when beaten by *Hawk High* in the 2014 *Fred Winter Juvenile Handicap Hurdle*. As for the remaining seven festival attempts by **Ballingarry**'s stock, no runner had managed to finish higher than seventh.

At last year's meeting, where four **Ballingarry** sired horses were entered for races, there was a big improvement in results. *Diego Du Charmil* won the *Fred Winter Juvenile Handicap Hurdle*; *Full Shift* picked up the last of the place dividends when finishing 4th in the *Brown Advisory & Merriebelle Stable Plate* and *Amigo* just missed out on the places when finishing 5th in the *Fulke Walwyn Kim Muir Challenge Cup Handicap Chase*. The only one of the four runners to let the side down was the aforementioned *Katgary*, who ran a wretched race and was eventually pulled up in the *Close Brothers Novices' Handicap Chase*.

With just twelve festival runs to go on, there is nowhere near enough data on which to make foolhardy conclusions, but the performances at the 2016 Cheltenham Festival certainly provides **Ballingarry** supporters with some encouragement for the future. It is interesting to note that the win and both places from the 12 festival runs were gained by horses who lined up at single figure odds. *Diego Du Charmil* had a starting price of 13/2 when winning last year's *Fred Winter*, and in the 2014 running of the race, *Katgary* claimed the runner-up spot at odds of 8/1. *Full Shift*'s 4th place finish in the aforementioned *Brown Advisory & Merriebelle Stable Plate* was secured at odds of 7/1. There have also been two occasions in which the **Ballingarry** bred runner started as the favourite for their festival debuts. *Balgarry*, was the very first of **Ballingarry**'s progeny to make a festival appearance, when he set off as the 6/1 joint favourite and finished seventh, in the 2012 *Coral Cup*. Two years later, and *Full Shift* made his festival debut in the 2014 *Martin Pipe Conditional Jockeys' Handicap Hurdle*. Despite being the 9/2 favourite for the race, the *Nicky Henderson* trained runner disappointed, and eventually finished well down the field in 11th. *Full Shift* tried his luck again in the following season's renewal of the race, this time racing at odds of 10/1. In reaching eighth spot, it was a marginally better performance.

Amigo's 5th in last year's *Kim Muir* is by far the best performance of the seven **Ballingarry** sired horses who have taken part in festival races at double figure odds. *Amigo*, a big priced 33/1 shot, was clear from his pursuers three from home, but had no extra to give towards the end of the race, when *Knock House* stayed on after the last to deny the *David Pipe* trained outsider a 4th place dividend.

In summary, what can we say? So far, anyone supporting the **Ballingarry** sired festival runners would have received a win or place dividend for 1 in every 4 runs from the progeny. Limiting any wagers to only those runners who went off at single figure odds would have yielded a return of £5.88 to a £1.00 each way stake. At this time, my initial instinct is that there will be further festival successes for the offspring, and so I am certainly not against anyone wanting to place a bet on **Ballingarry** bred runners at the 2017 Cheltenham Festival. That said, with just 12 festival runs to go on, the evidence on **Ballingarry**'s stock is inconclusive, and perhaps a more prudent approach is to maintain a watching brief.

Beneficial (GB)

Quote from the 2016 Cheltenham Festival Stallion Guide - "The sixteen **Beneficial** sired horses who lined up at last year's festival performed almost exactly in line with what I said about the progeny in the 2015 Cheltenham Festival Guide. Last year, I advised that I was not a fan of backing **Beneficial's** progeny at the Cheltenham Festival, as overall I considered the record to be very poor. So, what happened at the 2015 festival with the offspring's 16 runners? Two runners managed to achieve runner-up spots (more of that later), one horse finished fifth and the rest all finished 8th or worse."

Beneficial (Died as a 23-y-o in 2013)							
Race Format	*Miles*	*Won*	*Placed*	*Unplaced*	*Total*	*Win %*	*Place %*
	About 2m	0	0	7	7	0%	0%
Hurdles	About 2m 4f	1	2	13	16	6%	19%
	About 3m	1	0	6	7	14%	14%
	About 2m	0	4	13	17	0%	24%
Chases	About 2m 4f	1	0	9	10	10%	10%
	About 3m	3	3	18	24	13%	25%
	About 4m	0	1	9	10	0%	10%
Bumper	About 2m	0	1	4	5	0%	20%
Total		**6**	**11**	**79**	**96**	**6%**	**18%**

The last Cheltenham Festival winner from **Beneficial's** stock happened in 2014, when *Barry Geraghty* rode *More Of That* (15/2) to a 1½ length victory ahead of *Annie Power* in the *Ladbrokes World Hurdle*. Two years later, *More Of That* lined up in last season's *RSA Chase* as the 6/4 favourite, but having suffered broken blood vessels in the latter stages of the race, could only finish 3rd. A third place dividend, however, was better than the achievements of the other nine **Beneficial** sired horses that ran at the festival last year, where none of them managed a top eight finish. Not that I was surprised. The statistics are clear-cut. **Beneficial's** progeny have a dismal Cheltenham Festival record.

At the 2015 festival, 13 of the 16 **Beneficial** bred runners finished 8th or worse. And *More Of That's* success, highlighted above, was the sole win or place return from the 14 of the progeny that took part in the 2014 Cheltenham Festival. So, over the past three years, **Beneficial's** offspring have recorded *More Of That's* 1st and 3rd plus 2 runner-up spots from a total of 40 festival runners. Moreover, 31 of those 40 runners failed to trouble the judge, finishing 8th or worse.

When it comes to the Cheltenham Festival, my strong recommendation to punters is to ignore **Beneficial's** offspring completely unless there is a deluge of rain. In my view, it was heavy rain before Gold Cup day at the 2015 festival that was the critical factor in helping two of the four **Beneficial** bred runners, that raced that Friday, to record runner-up spots. There were two entries in the *St. James's Place Foxhunter Chase Challenge Cup*, one of whom was *Salsify* (10/1) who had already won the *Foxhunters* twice in 2012 and 2013. He was eventually pulled up in the race four from home, but the other **Beneficial** sired runner, *Following Dreams*, managed to finish second at the rewarding odds of 50/1, some 17 lengths behind the *Nina Carberry* ridden, *On The Fringe*. The other two of **Beneficial's** offspring to take part on the Friday were entered in the festival's final race - the *A.P. McCoy Grand Annual Chase Challenge Cup*, and it was the *Jonjo O'Neill* trained 12/1 shot, *Eastlake*, who finished runner-up four lengths behind *Next Sensation*. The other **Beneficial** bred runner, *Mount Colah* (25/1), was pulled up two from home when tailed off.

There was also an avalanche of rain at the Cheltenham Festival on Friday 15th March 2013, when **Beneficial**'s stock had seven race entries. The rain started lashing down from noon which resulted in the official going being changed to soft from the third race onwards. **Beneficial**'s offspring were represented with two runners in each of the last three races that day, and managed to record two victories and two placed efforts from the six runners who lined up. For the record, *Salsify* (2/1 favourite) won the *CGA Foxhunter Chase Challenge Cup*; *Salubrious* (16/1) won the *Martin Pipe Conditional Jockeys' Handicap Hurdle* with the second **Beneficial** bred runner, *Make Your Mark* securing the 4th place dividend at 8/1; And *Kid Cassidy* finished 2nd at 12/1 in the last race of the day, the *Johnny Henderson Grand Annual Chase Challenge Cup*.

Backing all eleven **Beneficial** sired runners, who ran on soft ground following the torrential downpours of 15th March 2013 and 13th March 2015, would have provided an excellent profit of £26.40 to a £1.00 each way stake. Compare this profit and the two wins and four places achieved, with the remainder of the progeny who took their chance in races when it hadn't been pouring with rain. Of the remaining 85 **Beneficial** bred contenders since the 2007 festival onwards, four have won and eight have secured a place dividend. Staking a £1.00 each way bet on all 85 of these runners would have delivered a rather painful £100.60 loss.

To add further evidence to my conviction that **Beneficial**'s offspring don't perform at Cheltenham Festivals unless there has been lots of rain, one only has to look at the starting prices of the seventeen **Beneficial** bred runners who, over the past decade, have won or been placed. Of the six runners that provided a return to punters in the wet, four of them lined up at double figure odds, including a 16/1 winner and a 50/1 runner-up. This is in stark contrast to the starting prices for the eleven of **Beneficial**'s progeny who secured a win or place dividend on drier ground, where only *Benefficient* (20/1) in winning the 2013 *Jewson Novices' Chase* provided punters with a double figure price return. Based on the fact that the other ten runners were at single figure odds, some punters may believe a profit is possible by supporting only those runners at the front of the betting market. But they would be wrong, as in addition to the ten horses that provided a return, there were another eleven Beneficial bred runners at single figure odds, that didn't. In fact, eight of this group of eleven couldn't even manage to finish in the top eight positions.

Whilst we are on the subject of shorter priced horses, and despite the analysis provided above, in my previous Stallion Guides, I advised that a profitable strategy was possible by supporting Beneficial's progeny in festival races over a distance of three miles, provided their odds were under 10/1. Preceding last year's Cheltenham Festival, this set of circumstances had only arisen on five occasions, but if one had placed a bet each time it had happened, it would have been highly profitable, as four of the five runners who fitted the profile won. *Cooldine* won the 2009 *RSA Chase*; *Salsify* won the *Foxhunter Chase* twice in 2012 and 2013; And *More Of That* won the 2014 *Ladbrokes World Hurdle*. The only one not to win, *Becauseicouldntsee*, was hardly disgraced. The chestnut gelding started at a price of 9/1 and finished runner-up to *Sunnyhillboy* in the 2012 *Fulke Walwyn Kim Muir Challenge Cup Handicap Chase*.

My confidence in recommending this strategy has been diluted somewhat because of the performances of *More Of That* and **Upswing** in two of the festival's three mile chases last season. As advised previously, the *Jonjo O'Neill* trained and *J P McManus* owned *More Of That* finished 3rd in last season's *RSA Chase* as the 6/4 favourite. And **Upswing** became the very first of **Beneficial**'s offspring, running in a 3m Cheltenham Festival race and at single figure odds, who didn't achieve at least a place dividend. Also trained by *Jonjo O'Neill*, **Upswing** went off at a price of 8/1 in the *Fulke Walwyn Kim Muir Challenge Cup Handicap Chase*, but never threatened the leaders, finishing ninth. Despite these two performances making me markedly more cautious, the record of four wins and two places from just seven runs is still a very good return. Indeed, backing every **Beneficial** sired festival entry to run over three miles with an SP of under 10/1 would have resulted in a £21.05 profit to a £1.00 each way stake.

In conclusion, despite the anomaly above, I will continue to strike a line through any of **Beneficial**'s offspring at Cheltenham Festivals, unless, of course, it has been raining heavily. If you are at the festival meeting come March 2017, standing in a bar, and feeling a little miserable as a result of being squashed amongst everyone else who are sheltering from the torrential rain, then my suggestion would be to have a look through your rain soaked race card and look for any **Beneficial** sired runner. When a deluge of rain falls at a Cheltenham Festival, **Beneficial**'s offspring often perform well, and any bets on the progeny may just provide you with a little ray of sunshine underneath the mass of black clouds above!

Cape Cross (IRE)

Cape Cross was not featured in the 2016 Cheltenham Festival Stallion Guide.

Cape Cross (23-y-o)

Race Format	Miles	Won	Placed	Unplaced	Total	Win %	Place %
	About 2m	0	1	10	11	0%	9%
Hurdles	About 2m 4f	0	1	3	4	0%	25%
	About 3m	0	0	1	1	0%	0%
	About 2m	0	0	0	0	-	-
Chases	About 2m 4f	0	0	1	1	0%	0%
	About 3m	0	0	0	0	-	-
	About 4m	0	0	0	0	-	-
Bumper	About 2m	0	0	0	0	-	-
Total		**0**	**2**	**15**	**17**	**0%**	**12%**

With my tongue firmly in cheek, I predict that there will be a **Cape Cross** sired outsider taking part in a 2017 Cheltenham Festival contest, who will run far better than the 100/1 odds would suggest, and record a placing. For anyone who likes a fun bet based on a quirky trend, this is for you! The closest that **Cape Cross**'s progeny have come to winning a festival race happened with the very first appearance of a **Cape Cross** sired runner at a Cheltenham Festival. The horse in question was *Artist's Muse*, trained by *Ted Walsh* and ridden by his son, *Ruby*, who finished 2nd at odds of 12/1 in the 2006 *Fred Winter Juvenile Novices' Handicap Hurdle*. We had to wait 7 years for the next festival placing by a **Cape Cross** bred runner, and it occurred in the 2013 *Vincent O'Brien County Handicap Hurdle*, when *Manyriverstocross* registered a third placing at odds of 25/1. The odds doubled and the number of years we had to wait for a third festival place halved, when *Sky Khan* (50/1) claimed 3rd spot in the 2016 *Martin Pipe Conditional Jockeys' Handicap Hurdle*. If you are still with me in my line of thinking, in chronological order we have had three place positions of 12/1 in 2006; 25/1 in 2013; and 50/1 in 2016. Hence, the wacky prediction of a 100/1 placing for a **Cape Cross** bred runner in 2017!

Cape Cross's progeny have registered 18 festival appearances, 17 of which have occurred in the past decade. Looking at the table of results, one may be forgiven for striking a line through any **Cape Cross** bred runners that are entered at the 2017 Cheltenham Festival, but in my opinion, that action may be a little too hasty. First and foremost, there has only been one race in which the **Cape Cross** sired runner raced at single figure odds, when *Manyriverstocross* finished 7th in the 2014 *Rewards4Racing Novices' Handicap Chase*, at odds of 17/2. Furthermore, for ten of the 18 runs, the **Cape Cross** representative lined up at odds of 22/1 or greater with six of those starting prices ranging between being 50/1 and 125/1. Taking into account this overall lack of market support for the offspring, three places from a total of 18 festival appearances doesn't read too badly, albeit that backing every **Cape Cross** festival runner to date would have produced a loss of £11.25 to a £1.00 each way stake. It should also be pointed out that 50% of the 18 festival appearances resulted in a top 7 finish, so six of the runners weren't too far away from adding to the progeny's current festival record of three place positions.

At last year's Cheltenham Festival, **Cape Cross** was represented with five runners and we have already highlighted the 3rd place achieved by the *Lucinda Russell* trained, *Sky Khan*, in the 2016

Martin Pipe Conditional Jockeys' Handicap Hurdle. The next best performance was from *Leoncavallo* (18/1), who finished 5th of 15 runners in the *JCB Triumph Hurdle*. "Also-Ran" is the most appropriate term that can be applied to the performances of the other three Cape Cross sired runners from last year.

In conclusion, when it comes to the 2017 Cheltenham Festival, there is very little data available on which to make any firm judgements as to the likely success or otherwise of **Cape Cross**'s progeny. I would not necessarily dissuade anyone from supporting the progeny, as one cannot be too negative about the achievement of 3 places from 18 runs, especially in light of the starting prices of 12/1, 25/1 and 50/1. That said, as far as **Cape Cross**'s stock goes, I will probably keep my money in my pocket for the time being. Unless, of course, I find a suitable 100/1 fun bet!

Definite Article (GB)

Quote from the 2016 Cheltenham Festival Stallion Guide - "The recommendation to punters is to draw a line through any **Definite Article** bred entries who line up at the 2016 Cheltenham Festival."

Definite Article (25-y-o)

Race Format	Miles	Won	Placed	Unplaced	Total	Win %	Place %
Hurdles	About 2m	0	0	1	1	0%	0%
	About 2m 4f	0	0	3	3	0%	0%
	About 3m	0	0	5	5	0%	0%
Chases	About 2m	0	0	2	2	0%	0%
	About 2m 4f	0	0	1	1	0%	0%
	About 3m	0	0	3	3	0%	0%
	About 4m	0	0	1	1	0%	0%
Bumper	About 2m	0	0	4	4	0%	0%
Total		**0**	**0**	**20**	**20**	**0%**	**0%**

Let's cut to the chase. In the past decade, **Definite Article**'s stock has been represented in twenty runs at Cheltenham Festivals. None have won. None have been placed. Since 2007, trainer *Paul Nicholls* and jockey *Ruby Walsh* have come closest to recording a place position for the progeny, when the combination had to settle for 5th place with their 3/1 favourite, *Definity*, in the 2011 *Centenary Novices' Handicap Chase*. What about the other 19 runners? One fell, six were pulled up, ten completed their races in 10th position or worse, and the other two managed to finish 7th. All of which is a rather depressing set of performances.

There was certainly more encouragement for supporters of **Definite Article** preceding 2007. In the progeny's other nine festival races which took place between 2002 and 2006, the results included a 4th, 5th, 6th and 8th as well as two winners at the 2006 festival, both of which were trained by *Nicky Henderson*. **Non So**'s 14/1 success in the 2m5f *Racing Post Plate* was followed up by *Greenhope*'s victory at 20/1, and over 2m½f, in the *Johnny Henderson Grand Annual Chase Challenge Cup Handicap*. Since *Greenhope*'s victory, however, results for **Definite Article**'s offspring have been abysmal.

I guess there is a possibility that the progeny's performances may improve to pre-2007 levels, but for now, there is only one conclusion to be made. Strike out all **Definite Article** bred entries who line up at the 2017 Cheltenham Festival.

Dom Alco (FR)

Quote from the 2016 Cheltenham Festival Stallion Guide - "Although over 2/3rds of **Dom Alco**'s Cheltenham Festival runs have taken place over the bigger obstacles, it is over hurdles where the statistics show the best results. Over the past decade, six of the ten runs over hurdles have resulted in a top six finish, including two wins and two runner-up spots."

Dom Alco (Died as a 23-y-o in 2010)							
Race Format	*Miles*	*Won*	*Placed*	*Unplaced*	*Total*	*Win %*	*Place %*
Hurdles	About 2m	1	0	2	3	33%	33%
	About 2m 4f	1	1	5	7	14%	29%
	About 3m	0	2	0	2	0%	100%
Chases	About 2m	0	0	2	2	0%	0%
	About 2m 4f	0	0	5	5	0%	0%
	About 3m	0	2	14	16	0%	13%
	About 4m	0	0	5	5	0%	0%
Bumper	About 2m	0	1	0	1	0%	100%
Total		**2**	**6**	**33**	**41**	**5%**	**20%**

In the past decade of Cheltenham Festivals, 20 of **Dom Alco**'s progeny have registered 41 runs between them, with seven of the offspring having raced at the festival on three or more occasions, these being, ***Al Ferof*** (5 runs), ***Neptune Collonges*** (4), ***Sire Collonges*** (4), ***Gevrey Chambertin*** (3), ***Naiad Du Misselot*** (3), ***New Alco*** (3) and ***Silviniaco Conti*** (3). With the exception of ***Al Ferof***, who has delivered a return for punters at two Cheltenham Festival meetings, no other **Dom Alco** bred competitor has managed to secure more than a single festival win or place.

The figures within the table at the top of the page hide the fact that more often than not, **Dom Alco**'s progeny tend to perform reasonably well at Cheltenham Festivals. But not well enough to win. At the past 10 festivals, twenty of the 41 runs have resulted in a top six finish, including two wins, five seconds, one third and no fewer than six fourth place finishes. I should add that two fallers would almost certainly have made it 22 top six finishes from the 41 runs had they managed to complete the Cheltenham course. ***Sirene D'Ainay*** was leading and travelling well when falling two out in the 2014 *OLBG Mares Hurdle*, although clearly open to debate whether she would have beaten the exceptional *Quevega*, who won this specific contest for the sixth time in a row. And in 2013, the *Paul Nicholls* trained, ***Silviniaco Conti*** was travelling well when falling three out in the *Betfred Cheltenham Gold Cup Chase*.

Having secured so many top six finishes, it is rather surprising that **Dom Alco**'s offspring have failed to record a single victory in the festival's chase events. Indeed, when it comes to the bigger obstacles, **Dom Alco**'s progeny have delivered a rather pathetic return of just two place positions from a total of 32 Cheltenham Festival chase entries. And last year, it was the same old story with no return on any bets, and yet two top six finishes from the three runs over fences. The two horses that managed a top six spot were both trained by *Paul Nicholls*. ***Vicente*** (14/1) finished two places outside of the paid dividends when securing fifth in the *146th Year of the National Hunt Chase Challenge Cup* and ***Al Ferof*** took 4th place in the Grade 1 *Ryanair Chase*, making it the sixth occasion in which **Dom Alco**'s offspring had been placed fourth in Cheltenham Festival chase events. Returning to *Paul Nicholls*, he trained the winner of the 2012 *John Smith's Grand National Chase*,

Neptune Collonges, who four years prior to that success, became only the second **Dom Alco** bred runner to secure a place dividend in a Cheltenham race over fences. It was quite a day for *Paul Nicholls*. He secured a 1-2-3 in the 2008 *Totesport Cheltenham Gold Cup Chase*, with **Neptune Collonges** finishing third behind the renowned duo of *Denman* and *Kauto Star* who finished 1st and 2nd respectively. The first, and only other, **Dom Alco** sired runner to achieve a place in a festival chase event was *New Alco*, who achieved the feat just three days before *Neptune Collonges'* placing in the aforementioned *Gold Cup*. *New Alco* secured the runner-up spot in the 2008 *William Hill Trophy Handicap Chase*.

When one looks at the results of **Dom Alco**'s stock at Cheltenham Festivals, I find it quite bizarre that in 32 races over fences, the offspring have a dismal place strike rate of 6% having achieved just two place positions. And yet, when it comes to the smaller obstacles, despite having been entered in just 13 hurdle races, **Dom Alco**'s progeny have achieved a win strike rate of 15% and a win and place strike rate of 46%. At the 2016 Cheltenham Festival, it was yet another *Paul Nicholls* trained horse, **Arpege D'Alene**, who helped to maintain the impressive hurdle strike rate for **Dom Alco** bred runners, when he finished runner-up to *Mall Dini* in the *Pertemps Network Final*. It was the third time that **Dom Alco**'s offspring had raced in a Cheltenham Festival three mile hurdle event and the third time that the outcome had been a placed dividend. *Tribal Venture* was the first of the progeny to line up at a Cheltenham Festival on 11th March 2003, and at just five years old, he took part in the same event in which **Arpege D'Alene** would run in 13 years later. Although beaten by just over 12 lengths, **Tribal Venture**, at odds of 33/1, ran a good race and managed to attain 3rd place under a patient ride from jockey, *Davy Russell*. With **Grand Crus** managing 2nd in the 2011 *Ladbrokes World Hurdle*, **Dom Alco** sired runners have a 100% place record in 3m hurdle events.

With **Dom Alco**'s passing in 2010, the progeny's runners are that little bit older hence the likelihood that at future Cheltenham Festivals, **Dom Alco** sired runners will invariably be entered in the longer distance chase events. I consider the offspring have been somewhat unfortunate not to have recorded a festival success over the larger obstacles and despite the current appalling strike rate, I wouldn't be in the least surprised to see a **Dom Alco** bred secure a chase victory before the end of this decade. When it comes to hurdles, I am guessing that any entries will be few and far between. Nevertheless, if we find any **Dom Alco** bred runners entered in the festival's hurdle events, then with a 46% win and place strike rate, punters should look at them very seriously. Finally, with a 100% record of securing a place dividend in the festival's 3m hurdle events, combined with the progeny's current age profile being the right fit for the race, I will be very interested in supporting any **Dom Alco** sired runner that lines up in the 2017 *Pertemps Final Handicap Hurdle*.

Dr Massini (IRE)

Quote from the 2016 Cheltenham Festival Stallion Guide - "From a punter's perspective, even though the strategy would consist of a general lack of drama and excitement, backing every runner sired by **Dr Massini**, over the past decade of Cheltenham Festivals, would have provided a rather healthy profit of £22.50 to a £1.00 each way stake."

Dr Massini (24-y-o)

Race Format	Miles	Won	Placed	Unplaced	Total	Win %	Place %
	About 2m	0	1	1	2	0%	50%
Hurdles	About 2m 4f	1	0	3	4	25%	25%
	About 3m	0	0	2	2	0%	0%
	About 2m	0	0	2	2	0%	0%
Chases	About 2m 4f	0	2	2	4	0%	50%
	About 3m	0	2	5	7	0%	29%
	About 4m	0	0	1	1	0%	0%
Bumper	About 2m	0	0	1	1	0%	0%
Total		**1**	**5**	**17**	**23**	**4%**	**26%**

With **Dr Massini**'s progeny, it is a case of boom or bust at the Cheltenham Festival. In the past decade, fifteen of the 17 unplaced horses finished outside the top six places, of which eleven were tenth or worse. There have only been two unplaced horses that have finished in the top six positions, and one of those occurred at last year's festival, when **Indian Castle** tackled the *Fulke Walwyn Kim Muir Challenge Cup Handicap Chase* for the second time, having finished 7th in the 2014 event, when going off as the 7/2 favourite. He did better in the 2016 renewal, but only just, attaining a 6th placing at the much bigger price of 16/1. The other of **Dr Massini**'s offspring to finish outside the places but in the top 6 was **Adrenalin Flight**, who in 2014 was beaten by less than one length in 4th at 100/1 in the four mile *Terry Biddlecombe National Hunt Chase Amateur Riders' Novices' Chase*.

Although there have been many inauspicious performances from the progeny of **Dr Massini**, every so often, we witness a very good performance and often at big prices. The most recent example occurred at the 2015 Cheltenham Festival, when trainer, *Ian Williams* elected to enter the aforementioned **Indian Castle** in the *Ultima Business Solutions Handicap Chase*. Having secured a place dividend by finishing 4th in the race, at odds of 16/1, the decision was clearly a good one.

Looking at the trends overall, in the past decade, **Dr Massini**'s offspring have had a total of 23 runs at the festival, which has resulted in one victory and five placed efforts. The winner came from **Massini's Maguire**, trained by *Philip Hobbs*, who sprang a surprise when *Richard Johnson* rode him to victory in the 2007 *Ballymore Properties Novices' Hurdle* at 20/1. Two years later, the same horse took part at half those odds (10/1) in the *RSA Chase* and managed to take third place, despite being some 25 lengths behind the winner. The shortest priced placed horse was **Psycho** who started as the 5/1 favourite in the 2008 *Vincent O'Brien County Handicap Hurdle*, running well to finish runner-up to 50/1 shot, *Silver Jaro*. Following some more disheartening performances in 2010 and 2011, it was in 2012, three years after **Massini's Maguire**'s third in the *RSA Chase*, that the progeny once again achieved a place dividend, this time in the 2012 *Byrne Group Plate* when **Glam Gerry** at 33/1 ran into third spot. The following year, **Changing Times** at the huge price of 100/1 finished 3rd in the 2013 *Jewson Novices' Chase*.

If one had backed all of **Dr Massini**'s offspring that had taken part in Cheltenham Festivals, then it would have produced a profit of £20.50 to a £1.00 each way stake, so one cannot argue on supporting the progeny at the 2017 Cheltenham Festival. However, as mentioned earlier, the progeny do have a boom and bust track record, and so whilst supporters patiently wait for their winnings in roughly every fourth race, for the races in between, they will have to contend with an element of boredom as they watch their **Dr Massini** bred selection finish down the field.

Flemensfirth (USA)

Quote from the 2016 Cheltenham Festival Stallion Guide - "Sadly, the 2015 festival provided us with more of the same, and yet another dismal set of results for the progeny. For the record, twelve **Flemensfirth** sired horses lined up last season, of which only two managed to secure a top six position, resulting in the depressing coincidence that, for the second year in a row, ten runners failed to finish higher than ninth."

Flemensfirth (25-y-o)							
Race Format	*Miles*	*Won*	*Placed*	*Unplaced*	*Total*	*Win %*	*Place %*
Hurdles	About 2m	0	0	4	4	0%	0%
	About 2m 4f	0	5	15	20	0%	25%
	About 3m	0	2	9	11	0%	18%
Chases	About 2m	1	0	2	3	33%	33%
	About 2m 4f	2	2	8	12	17%	33%
	About 3m	1	2	16	19	5%	16%
	About 4m	0	2	13	15	0%	13%
Bumper	About 2m	0	0	8	8	0%	0%
Total		**4**	**13**	**75**	**92**	**4%**	**18%**

Who is the stallion, whose offspring recorded 5 winners and 8 places from 36 Cheltenham Festival races for the six years between 2005 and 2010, resulting in a profit of £64.80 to a £1.00 each way stake had one backed all 36 runners? And a second question. Who is the stallion, whose offspring recorded six places and zero wins from 61 Cheltenham Festival races for the six years between 2011 and 2016, resulting in a loss of £88.20 to a £1.00 each way stake had one backed all 61 runners? The answer to both questions is **Flemensfirth** and I'm at a loss to understand why the incredible turnaround in fortunes. Perhaps some 14 or 15 years ago, the stud manager at *Coolmore's Beeches Stud* in Ireland changed **Flemensfirth**'s diet!

At the 2016 Cheltenham Festival, it was another set of dismal results for **Flemensfirth**'s stock. Twelve **Flemensfirth** sired horses lined up last year, of which only two could manage a top six position. It is becoming a rather freakish and depressing trend that for each of the past three years, precisely ten of the **Flemensfirth** bred entries to have taken part at each Cheltenham Festival have been unable to finish higher than eighth. In total, from the 2014 Cheltenham Festival onwards, **Flemensfirth**'s offspring have lined up in 35 races of which we have witnessed two runner-up spots, a 4th, 5th and 6th and a further 30 horses that were nowhere to be seen.

At the 2014 Cheltenham Festival, best of the eleven **Flemensfirth** bred runners was *Sizing Gold,* who finished sixth in the *JLT Novices' Chase* over 2½ miles. In 2015, *Noble Endeavor*'s effort in the *Martin Pipe Conditional Jockeys' Handicap Hurdle* was the closest the progeny have come to delivering the first **Flemensfirth** sired winner since *Paddy Brennan* rode *Imperial Commander* to victory over the *Paul Nicholls* trained pair of *Kauto Star* and *Denman* in what was a memorable 2010 *Totesport Cheltenham Gold Cup Chase*. Even though *Noble Endeavor* had taken a narrow advantage in the final 100 yards of the race, the *Gordon Elliott* trained 14/1 gelding failed to hold on from the rallying *Killultagh Vic*, who just got up in the final stride to win by a head. Last season, it was a 66/1 shot that managed to provide **Flemensfirth** supporters with a winning each way bet for only the second time in three years, when the *Jessica Harrington* trained, **Rock On The Moor** finished a well beaten runner-up to the 4/6 odds-on favourite, *Vroum Vroum Mag*, in the 2016 *OLBG Mares' Hurdle*.

Even though the performances from **Flemensfirth**'s offspring may have been encouraging preceding 2011, the current advice to punters could not be more emphatic. Steer clear of the progeny until we see a clear turnaround in recent trends.

Fragrant Mix (IRE)

Fragrant Mix was not featured in the 2016 Cheltenham Festival Stallion Guide.

Fragrant Mix (23-y-o)

Race Format	Miles	Won	Placed	Unplaced	Total	Win %	Place %
Hurdles	About 2m	0	2	0	2	0%	100%
	About 2m 4f	0	1	0	1	0%	100%
	About 3m	0	1	0	1	0%	100%
Chases	About 2m	0	0	0	0	-	-
	About 2m 4f	1	1	1	3	33%	67%
	About 3m	0	0	1	1	0%	0%
	About 4m	0	0	1	1	0%	0%
Bumper	About 2m	0	0	0	0	-	-
Total		**1**	**5**	**3**	**9**	**11%**	**67%**

With only nine runs on which to make any analysis, and with just one solitary representative in each of the past four festival meetings, it is perhaps debateable why I have included Fragrant Mix in the 2017 Cheltenham Festival Stallion Guide. Moreover, it may well happen again, that come March, amongst the several hundred festival entries, there is just one that has Fragrant Mix listed as the sire. Against this background, should one turn the page and start reading about *Galileo*? My advice is to carry on reading, because if you find a Fragrant Mix sired runner at the 2017 Cheltenham Festival, then the compelling evidence suggests that you should place a great big each way bet on it.

If you had placed a £1.00 each way bet on all of Fragrant Mix sired runners who have appeared at a Cheltenham Festival, then you would have made a profit of £27.20 and collected a return on six of your nine bets. Putting aside the runs of *Quolibet* (50/1) in the 2011 *Glenfarclas Handicap Chase* and *Relax* (12/1) in the 2013 *Fulke Walwyn Kim Muir Challenge Cup Handicap Chase*, where both runners were pulled up, the other seven appearances from the offspring have resulted in a top four finish. And the starting prices have been very satisfactory; a 16/1 winner; three runner-up spots of 14/1, 16/1 and 33/1; a 7/1 3rd place; a 4th place paid dividend at 14/1; and a 33/1 fourth placing that was outside the paid dividend places.

I predict that the name "*Uxizandre*" will be said out loud in sporting quizzes up and down the country for many years to come. The question posed is unlikely to be, "What is the only horse sired by Fragrant Mix to win at a Cheltenham Festival?", because not only will that be a very hard question for most people to answer, but there is a strong chance, in my view, that Fragrant Mix may well produce another festival winner. More likely, the question will be, "What horse provided Tony McCoy with his last ever Cheltenham Festival winner?" I was lucky enough to back *Uxizandre* in the 2015 *Ryanair Chase* where A P McCoy rode the 16/1 chance in front from start to finish, finding extra approaching the last fence, and then going clear from runner-up *Ma Filleule*, to win by 5 lengths. The previous year in the *JLT Novices' Chase*, at the rewarding odds of 33/1, *Uxizandre* finished runner-up to *Taquin Du Seuil*, beaten by less than a length.

Going back to the early part of this decade, the first couple of Fragrant Mix bred racehorses to appear at a Cheltenham Festival were *Radium* and *Son Amix*, both of whom registered a 14/1 place dividend in two of the hurdle events at the 2010 meeting. Following their satisfactory debuts, both horses were entered to take part at the 2011 Festival. *Son Amix*, trained by *Thomas Cooper* in Ireland, improved on his 4th placing in the 2010 *Fred Winter Juvenile Novices' Handicap Hurdle*, by going up a mile in distance the following season, to clinch the runner-up spot in the 3m *Pertemps Final*. In contrast, the *Nicky Henderson* trained **Radium**, was unable to improve on his 2nd in the 2010 *Martin Pipe Conditional Jockeys' Handicap Hurdle*, when at the next festival, he finished 4th and just outside the places, at 33/1, in the *Jewson Novices' Chase*.

At last year's meeting, following **Uxizandre**'s 2nd in 2014 and victory in 2015, it was down to the grey mare, **Bloody Mary**, to see if **Fragrant Mix**'s progeny could secure a win or place from their sole Cheltenham Festival representative for three years running. **Bloody Mary**, trained by *Nicky Henderson*, was the 7/1 3rd favourite for the first ever running of the *Dawn Run Mares' Novices Hurdle*, a race sponsored last year by *Trull House Stud*. The *Willie Mullins* trained *Limini*, the 8/11 odds on favourite, was widely regarded as the likely winner for this Grade 2 event over 2m1f, and the market was proved correct as *Ruby Walsh* rode the chestnut mare to an impressive victory, with **Bloody Mary**, some 7 lengths behind the winner, coming home in third.

In summary, although there have been very few of **Fragrant Mix**'s progeny entered at jump racing's showpiece event, so far punters have collected a return for two in every three each way bets. While it may be rather disconcerting to offer an opinion based on an inadequate number of festival runs, I will let my heart rule my head and encourage punters to back **Fragrant Mix**'s offspring at the 2017 Cheltenham Festival.

Galileo (IRE)

Quote from the 2016 Cheltenham Festival Stallion Guide - "**Galileo**'s stock typically don't perform when it comes to tackling the Cheltenham hurdles."

Race Format	Miles	Won	Placed	Unplaced	Total	Win %	Place %
					Galileo (19-y-o)		
Hurdles	About 2m	1	1	16	18	6%	11%
	About 2m 4f	1	0	7	8	13%	13%
	About 3m	0	1	4	5	0%	20%
Chases	About 2m	0	0	0	0	-	-
	About 2m 4f	0	0	0	0	-	-
	About 3m	0	0	0	0	-	-
	About 4m	0	0	0	0	-	-
Bumper	About 2m	0	0	2	2	0%	0%
Total		**2**	**2**	**29**	**33**	**6%**	**12%**

Apart from two sixth place efforts in the *Weatherbys Champion Bumper*, all of the other **Galileo** bred festival entries have raced exclusively in Cheltenham's hurdle events, numbering 31 runs in total. For the most part, anyone who had backed **Galileo**'s offspring in those 31 hurdle races would have been disappointed, as only two horses have managed to win or place. Moreover, in about 2/3rds of the races (20 of 31), **Galileo** sired runners failed to finish in the top eight positions.

The stand out hurdler of **Galileo**'s stock is *Celestial Halo* who raced six times at the Cheltenham Festival and rewarded punters with a victory or runner-up spot on three occasions. He provided owner *Andy Stewart* with his first ever festival winner by taking the 2008 *JCB Triumph Hurdle*, before finishing runner-up the following season in the 2009 *Smurfit Kappa Champion Hurdle Challenge Trophy*, beaten just a neck by the *Nicky Henderson* trained, *Punjabi*. In 2010, he attempted the *Champion Hurdle* again, but this time finished a well beaten fourth. Having finished down the field in the 2012 *Stan James Champion Hurdle Challenge Trophy*, he attempted three miles for the first time in the *Ladbrokes World Hurdle* in 2013. Although unfancied at 40/1, he ran another cracking race (except for blundering the last) to finish runner-up to the *Charles Byrnes* trained, *Solwhit*. In 2014, this grand servant from the *Paul Nicholls* yard had his sixth run at the Cheltenham Festival, running in the *Ladbrokes World Hurdle* for a second time. On this occasion, however, *Celestial Halo* finished last of the ten runners, after which the decision was made to retire him.

The only other **Galileo** bred horse to record a win at a Cheltenham Festival is **Windsor Park**, who won the 2015 *Neptune Investment Management Novices' Hurdle* at odds of 9/2. Ridden by *Davy Russell*, and trained by *Dermot Weld*, **Windsor Park** was up with the leaders throughout, before running on well after the last, to win quite comfortably from runner-up *Parlour Games*.

Having had five runners at the 2015 Cheltenham Festival, it was somewhat of a surprise, to see only one of **Galileo**'s offspring appear at jump racing's showpiece last year. Trained by *Henry De Bromhead*, **Supasundae** was the sole representative, appearing in the 2016 *Sky Bet Supreme Novices' Hurdle* and finishing in seventh at odds of 12/1. The previous season, in only his third race, **Supasundae** led for much of the way in the *Weatherbys Champion Bumper*, before fading just over a furlong out to finish sixth.

With **Galileo** being a young stallion at 19 years old, there is a good chance that at forthcoming Cheltenham Festivals, every so often, one of his offspring will pop up out of the blue and record a festival win or place. However, for every winner, there will be a whole bunch of losers, many of which will finish well down the field and be listed as "also ran" in racing commentaries. The fact is that supporting **Galileo** sired runners at Cheltenham Festivals has been highly unprofitable. Backing all 33 runners would have resulted in a loss of £21.50 to a £1.00 win stake or a loss of £38.90 if backing the progeny at £1.00 each way. Come the festival in March, my advice is to disregard all **Galileo** sired entries.

Germany (USA)

Quote from the 2016 Cheltenham Festival Stallion Guide - "60% of **Germany**'s offspring entered in March's National Hunt showpiece festival have been victorious."

Germany (Died as a 22-y-o in 2013)

Race Format	Miles	Won	Placed	Unplaced	Total	Win %	Place %
Hurdles	About 2m	2	0	2	4	50%	50%
	About 2m 4f	1	0	0	1	100%	100%
	About 3m	0	0	0	0	-	-
Chases	About 2m	1	1	4	6	17%	33%
	About 2m 4f	0	0	0	0	-	-
	About 3m	0	0	0	0	-	-
	About 4m	0	0	0	0	-	-
Bumper	About 2m	0	0	0	0	-	-
Total		**4**	**1**	**6**	**11**	**36%**	**45%**

The table above provides the results on how **Germany**'s progeny have performed in the past 10 years of Cheltenham Festivals, and so does not encompass *Tiger Cry*'s 2nd placing in the 2006 *Johnny Henderson Grand Annual Chase Challenge Cup*, which was the very first appearance of **Germany**'s offspring at a festival meeting. If we include *Tiger Cry*'s 2006 race, then **Germany**'s stock have only appeared in a total of twelve festival races. There are a few stallions within this Guide whose brood have yet to win a festival race and several more whose progeny have collected just 1 or 2 victories, and yet the vast majority have had more than 12 festival runs. So, it is some feat that **Germany**'s brood have registered four festival successes, or simply put one victory in every three festival appearances.

The 12 festival appearances are down to just five of **Germany**'s progeny, and another exceptional statistic to bear in mind, is that only two of those five have so far failed to win a Cheltenham Festival event. Put another way, all six win and place positions, have been recorded by just three **Germany** sired runners, these being *Captain Cee Bee* (4 runs), *Tiger Cry* (3 runs) and *Faugheen* (2 runs). *Tiger Cry*, trained by *Arthur Moore*, specialised in the two mile *Grand Annual Chase*. As highlighted earlier, he was runner-up in 2006, went one better to win the prize two years later, and then finished fifth in 2009, just a nose away from 4th and a paid dividend place. *Captain Cee Bee*, owned by *J P McManus*, ran all his four races over the minimum trip of two miles. He won the *Anglo Irish Bank Supreme Novices' Hurdle* in 2008, finished 8th in the 2010 *Irish Independent Arkle Challenge Trophy Chase*, secured 3rd in the *sportingbet.com Queen Mother Champion Chase* in 2011 and finally, at the grand old age of thirteen (hence the 100/1 odds), ran fantastically well to finish fifth in the 2014 *Stan James Champion Hurdle Challenge Trophy*.

At the end of January last year, *Faugheen* won his 12th National Hunt race under Rules in the *BHP Insurances Irish Champion Hurdle* at *Leopardstown*. He beat his stablemate, *Arctic Fire* by 15 lengths and won easily. It was widely anticipated that *Faugheen* would win the 2016 *Stan James Champion Hurdle Challenge Trophy*, repeating his 2015 success in the race, when on 17th February 2016, his trainer *Willie Mullins* announced that one of his biggest stars would miss the race due to a sore suspensory ligament injury. At the time of writing, *Faugheen* hasn't raced since, although *Willie Mullins* is hopeful that the 9 year old gelding will return to action at *Leopardstown* to defend his *BHP*

Irish Champion Hurdle crown on 29th January 2017. As it stands in mid-January, **Faugheen** is currently the favourite for the 2017 *Champion Hurdle* and like most racing fans, I sincerely hope that *Willie Mullins* can get him fit and ready for the festival's showpiece hurdle event.

Faugheen was the one and only **Germany** sired representative at the Cheltenham Festival in 2015. It was his second run at the festival and he did not disappoint supporters or odds-on favourite backers, as he quickened when it mattered and kept on well up the hill, to win the *Stan James Champion Hurdle Challenge Trophy* by 1½ lengths, from stablemates *Arctic Fire* and the eleven year old legend, *Hurricane Fly*. To date, **Faugheen** stands alone as the only one of the progeny to have run in a festival event at a distance other than two miles. Not that it mattered. **Faugheen** was well fancied as the 6/4 favourite in the 2014 *Neptune Investment Management Novices' Hurdle* over 2m5f, and he romped home to victory under *Ruby Walsh* by 4½ lengths from *Ballyalton*.

With **Faugheen** being absent from the 2016 Cheltenham Festival, it was left to **Germany Calling** to be the sole **Germany** sired representative last year, and the 33/1 *Charlie Longsdon* trained outsider made his appearance in the very last race of the meeting, when finishing 17th of 24 runners in the *Johnny Henderson Grand Annual Chase Challenge Cup*. It was **Germany Calling**'s second festival appearance and the second time that he had finished 17th! On the first occasion, at odds of 100/1, he finished just one from last in a field of 18, in the 2014 *Sky Bet Supreme Novices' Hurdle*. **Fighting Chance** is the fifth of **Germany**'s progeny to have raced at a Cheltenham Festival and he disappointed when he was pulled up before three out in the 2010 running of the *Grand Annual Chase*.

With just 12 festival appearances from **Germany**'s progeny in eleven years, it is unrealistic to expect anything more than say two or three **Germany** sired entries at the 2017 Cheltenham Festival. A much more realistic expectation, however, is a fifth Cheltenham festival success for the offspring, with **Faugheen**, of course, being the most likely to deliver the goods.

Gold Well (GB)

Quote from the 2016 Cheltenham Festival Stallion Guide - "The festival's opening handicap race, a Grade 3 chase run over a distance of 3m½f, has been a successful event over the past two years for **Gold Well**'s supporters."

Gold Well (16-y-o)							
Race Format	_Miles_	_Won_	_Placed_	_Unplaced_	_Total_	_Win %_	_Place %_
Hurdles	About 2m	0	0	0	0	-	-
	About 2m 4f	0	1	1	2	0%	50%
	About 3m	1	0	1	2	50%	50%
Chases	About 2m	0	0	0	0	-	-
	About 2m 4f	0	1	3	4	0%	25%
	About 3m	1	2	1	4	25%	75%
	About 4m	0	0	2	2	0%	0%
Bumper	About 2m	0	0	1	1	0%	0%
Total		**2**	**4**	**9**	**15**	**13%**	**40%**

In last year's Stallion Guide, despite there being only 11 races on which to make any judgement, I advised that there were encouraging early signals of **Gold Well**'s progeny performing well at Cheltenham Festival meetings. My gut feeling was that further festival successes would follow and last year's four runs from the offspring provided additional evidence that **Gold Well** is a stallion to look out for at the 2017 Cheltenham Festival. And the starting point for punters is to see if there is a **Gold Well** bred entry amongst the list of runners in the festival's opening handicap event, the _Ultima Handicap Steeple Chase_.

Referring to the quote at the top of the page, the _Ultima Handicap Steeple Chase_ is a Grade 3 event run over a distance of 3m½f, and for the past three years, a **Gold Well** sired runner has finished 1st or 2nd in the race. At odds of 10/1, **Holywell** won the then named _Baylis & Harding Affordable Luxury Handicap Chase_ in 2014, beating _Ma Filleule_ by 1¾ lengths. In 2015, _Ultima Business Solution Ltd_ took on sponsorship of the race, in which **Grand Jesture** lined up in an attempt to make it two consecutive victories in the race for **Gold Well**'s offspring. It was a gallant effort by the _Henry De Bromhead_ trained 25/1 shot, who ran well and stayed on at the finish, but was always held by _The Druids Nephew_, who won the event by 3¾ lengths. Last season, **Holywell** returned to take part in this race, having finished a very respectable 4th in the preceding season's _Betfred Cheltenham Gold Cup Chase_. His attempt in the 2016 _Ultima Handicap Chase_, to make it 2 wins from 2 runs, was thwarted by the _David Pipe_ trained, _Un Temps Pour Tout_ who won readily by 7 lengths, leaving **Holywell** to pick up the runner-up spot.

In addition to **Holywell**, **Gold Well** was represented by three other runners at the 2016 Cheltenham Festival, and another placing was recorded for the progeny when **Legacy Gold**, trained by _Stuart Crawford_, stayed on to take 3rd spot, at the very rewarding odds of 40/1 in the _OLBG Mares' Hurdle_. **Legacy Gold**'s jockey was _Andrew Lynch_, whose biggest riding success was in riding the _Henry de Bromhead_ trained _Sizing Europe_ to victory in the _Sportingbet.com Queen Mother Champion Chase_ in 2011. _Andrew Lynch_ rode his second **Gold Well** sired horse at last year's festival in Cheltenham's Cross Country race, the _Glenfarclas Chase_. On this occasion, however, the jockey was unable to get into the places, and his horse, *Ballyboker Bridge* (16/1) finished 6th, later promoted to 5th, following the disqualification of the on the day 'winner', *Any Currency*.

Taking all 15 runs to date, **Gold Well** supporters have watched the offspring build up a highly impressive Cheltenham Festival record, registering a top six finishing position on two in every three races, and being rewarded with a win or place on six occasions. And for anyone who had backed all 15 runners, the rewards have been significant, producing a profit of £40.25 to a £1.00 each way stake. To be fair, most of that profit is down to the *Jonjo O'Neill* trained, *Holywell*, who is responsible for the progeny's two Cheltenham Festival victories. We have already highlighted the second of those wins, when *Richie McLernon* rode the 10/1 chance to victory in the 2014 *Baylis & Harding Affordable Luxury Handicap Chase*. And it was the same jockey who was on board for *Holywell*'s first festival success, which occurred over hurdles in the 2013 *Pertemps Final*. Blinkered for the first time, *Holywell* (25/1) won comfortably by 1½ lengths from the staying on *Captain Sunshine*.

Like *Holywell*, *John's Spirit*, also from the *Jonjo O'Neill* stable, is another of **Gold Well**'s offspring to have run in the last four Cheltenham Festivals. Although *John's Spirit* disappointed as the 11/2 joint favourite in last season's visit to Cheltenham in the *Brown Advisory & Merriebelle Stable Plate*, the horse had run respectably in his three previous festival races, securing a 4th place dividend in the 2014 *Byrne Group Plate* and finishing 5th and 7th in his other two races. As with *Holywell*, *Richie McLernon* was the jockey for all four of *John's Spirit*'s festival races, so if we include *Mr Watson*'s pulled up result in the 2013 *Coral hurdle*, then *Mr McLernon* has been the jockey, and *Jonjo O'Neill* the trainer, for 9 of the 15 festival appearances of **Gold Well**'s stock.

In looking forward to the 2017 Cheltenham Festival, my conclusion is that we should be interested in supporting **Gold Well** sired runners. Clearly, we need to be a little cautious, as the progeny have amassed just 15 festival appearances, and eight of those are down to just two horses, these being *John's Spirit* and *Holywell*, the latter of which has been responsible for the two festival victories. Nevertheless, to date, **Gold Well**'s offspring have an impressive set of festival statistics with 66% of the runners hitting a top 6 finish, 40% of the runners rewarding punters with a win or place dividend and a profit of £40.25 to a £1.00 each way stake for backing all 15 of **Gold Well** sired participants. Year after year, the evidence is mounting that horses sired by **Gold Well** perform well at Cheltenham Festivals.

Hernando (FR)

Quote from the 2016 Cheltenham Festival Stallion Guide - "The strong advice to punters is to ignore any **Hernando** sired runner who lines up in a festival race labelled as an outsider."

Hernando (Died as a 23-y-o in 2013)

Race Format	Miles	Won	Placed	Unplaced	Total	Win %	Place %
Hurdles	About 2m	0	0	8	8	0%	0%
	About 2m 4f	0	1	6	7	0%	14%
	About 3m	1	0	7	8	13%	13%
Chases	About 2m	0	0	0	0	-	-
	About 2m 4f	0	0	2	2	0%	0%
	About 3m	0	0	3	3	0%	0%
	About 4m	0	0	0	0	-	-
Bumper	About 2m	0	0	2	2	0%	0%
Total		**1**	**1**	**28**	**30**	**3%**	**7%**

In analysing the statistics of **Hernando's** offspring at the Cheltenham Festival, it is the runner's starting price that appears to be the critical factor in determining any significant conclusions. In the past decade, there have been 23 horses fathered by **Hernando** at odds of 16/1 or greater and only two have managed to finish in the top eight finishing positions. The best performing longshot was the *Charlie Longsdon* trained, *Songe*, who finished 4th at 25/1 when well ridden by *Tom Siddall*, in the 2008 *JCB Triumph Hurdle*, run over a distance of 2m1f. In the same year, and next best, is *One Gulp* who at 50/1 finished 7th over three miles in the *Albert Bartlett Novices' Hurdle*.

So, over the past ten years, and having discounted the outsiders, we are left with seven **Hernando** bred runners with odds of 14/1 or less. The difference in the performances of these seven entries, and the results, are noticeably eye-catching as all seven recorded a top six finish. And in the case of **Hernando's** offspring, we shouldn't confuse "shorter-price" with odds-on shots, favourites, and for the most part, even single figure odds. In fact, five of these seven runners lined up with a starting price of between 12/1 and 14/1, one of which was victorious and another achieving a place dividend. The winner was the *Malcolm Jefferson* trained, *Cape Tribulation,* who took the *Pertemps Final* in 2012, at odds of 14/1. In the same year, *Make A Track*, at 12/1, picked up a 4th place dividend in the *Martin Pipe Conditional Jockeys' Handicap Hurdle*.

Cape Tribulation appeared at the Cheltenham Festival on five occasions, and on the three occasions when his starting price was 14/1 or less, the bay gelding achieved a top six finish. On top of his *Pertemps Final* victory, *Cape Tribulation* also managed two fifth place efforts in the 2009 *Albert Bartlett Novices' Hurdle* and the 2013 *Betfred Cheltenham Gold Cup Chase*. Incidentally, the only other **Hernando** sired Cheltenham Festival winner occurred 12 years ago when *No Refuge* won the 2005 *Royal & SunAlliance Novices' Hurdle* at odds of 17/2.

In summary, the strong advice is to ignore any **Hernando** sired runner who lines up in a festival race at odds of 16/1 or greater. However, if any of the offspring are shorter in price, 14/1 or less, then punters can at least expect a run for their money and a top six finish. For the record, over the past decade, adopting this approach would have resulted in just seven bets but a profit of £9.50 to a £1.00 each way stake.

Heron Island (IRE)

Quote from the 2016 Cheltenham Festival Stallion Guide - "Based on the 21 runs to date, **Heron Island**'s offspring have landed just three place positions at the festival in the past decade, so the early signs are not encouraging."

Heron Island (Died as a 15-y-o in 2008)

Race Format	Miles	Won	Placed	Unplaced	Total	Win %	Place %
	About 2m	0	0	2	2	0%	0%
Hurdles	About 2m 4f	0	1	2	3	0%	33%
	About 3m	0	2	3	5	0%	40%
	About 2m	0	0	1	1	0%	0%
Chases	About 2m 4f	1	0	1	2	50%	50%
	About 3m	0	1	6	7	0%	14%
	About 4m	0	0	0	0	-	-
Bumper	About 2m	0	0	3	3	0%	0%
Total		**1**	**4**	**18**	**23**	**4%**	**22%**

The 2016 Cheltenham Festival was a great success for **Heron Island**'s stock. From just two entries at last year's extravaganza, the progeny achieved a place dividend as well as securing a first ever Cheltenham Festival winner. These performances followed on from a disheartening set of results in 2015, where from eight runs, the best that the offspring could attain was a 5th place when *If In Doubt* (12/1) finished fifth of eight runners in the *RSA Chase*. *If In Doubt* had two more runs over fences following the Cheltenham race, when pulled up in both the *Boylesports Irish Grand National Chase* at *Fairyhouse* and the *Hennessy Gold Cup Chase* at *Newbury*, after which the *Philip Hobbs* trained gelding, was reverted back to hurdling. The decision clearly paid off, as jockey *Richard Johnson*, rode *If In Doubt* (10/1) within a length of the winner, when finishing 3rd in the 2016 *Pertemps Network Final*. It was the horse's third Cheltenham Festival run and his second appearance in the *Pertemps Network Final* race, as in the 2014 contest, this time ridden by *A P McCoy*, *If In Doubt* could only manage ninth.

The only other **Heron Island** sired contestant at the festival last year was also having his third race at a Cheltenham Festival, the *Willie Mullins* trained, **Black Hercules**. On his festival debut, **Black Hercules** ran well to gain 4th spot in the *Weatherbys Champion Bumper*, before lining up as the 5/2 favourite in the 2015 *Albert Bartlett Novices' Hurdle* where under a patient ride by *Ruby Walsh*, he could only finish seventh. Both horse and jockey paired up again in last season's *JLT Novices' Chase* and it was third time lucky for **Black Hercules**, as he stayed on well after narrowly leading at the last, to win by three lengths from *Bristol de Mai*, and so become the very first of **Heron Island**'s offspring to record a Cheltenham Festival victory.

Up until last year, **Heron Island**'s progeny had landed just three place positions at Cheltenham Festivals. *Galaxy Rock* (18/1) finished 4th in the 2011 *Fulke Walwyn Kim Muir Challenge Cup*, **Rathvinden** (11/2) took 3rd spot in the 2014 *Neptune Investment Management Novices' Hurdle* and in the same year, **Trustan Times**, even though less than one length behind the winner in a close finish, was placed 4th in the *Pertemps Network Final* at odds of 33/1. Having recorded just three places from 21 festival runs, in last year's Stallion Guide, I advised punters to avoid **Heron Island**'s progeny until there was any evidence to the contrary, and with the victory and third place from two runs at the 2016 festival, some considered re-analysis is needed.

Although there was an upturn in festival performances from **Heron Island**'s stock at the 2016 meeting, I doubt that this is the beginning of a trend that will continue into the 2017 Cheltenham Festival. Nevertheless, it is unwise to make any sound predictions based upon just 23 festival runs, where no specific race category stands out as particularly positive or negative, and so if you happen to strongly fancy a **Heron Island** bred runner come the spring, then I would not dissuade you from placing your bet. The simple truth remains, however, that if one had placed a £1.00 each way bet on all 23 of **Heron Island**'s offspring that had raced at a Cheltenham Festival, the outcome would be a loss of £18.85. With this negative being central to my thinking, and despite the possibility of a second festival victory not being totally out of the question, my advice remains consistent. Punters should be wary of supporting **Heron Island** bred runners at the 2017 Cheltenham Festival.

High Chaparral (IRE)

High Chaparral was not featured in the 2016 Cheltenham Festival Stallion Guide.

High Chaparral (Died as a 15-y-o in 2014)							
Race Format	_Miles_	_Won_	_Placed_	_Unplaced_	_Total_	_Win %_	_Place %_
	About 2m	2	0	11	13	15%	15%
Hurdles	About 2m 4f	0	0	0	0	-	-
	About 3m	0	0	1	1	0%	0%
	About 2m	0	0	0	0	-	-
Chases	About 2m 4f	0	0	0	0	-	-
	About 3m	0	1	1	2	0%	50%
	About 4m	0	0	0	0	-	-
Bumper	About 2m	0	0	1	1	0%	0%
Total		**2**	**1**	**14**	**17**	**12%**	**18%**

Only two of **High Chaparral**'s progeny have raced at a Cheltenham Festival where the starting prices for the runners have been under 10/1, and both horses hailed from _Nicky Henderson_'s Upper Lambourn yard, in Berkshire. One of those horses, **Altior**, at 4/1, ran in the opening race of last year's meeting in the _Sky Bet Supreme Novices' Hurdle_, and the second favourite was very impressive, quickening clear after the last, to win by seven lengths ahead of the 15/8 favourite, _Min_.

The other **High Chaparral** bred horse who has raced at the festival whilst being towards the front of the betting market, is **Hadrian's Approach**, who has twice appeared at the festival with a starting price of under 10/1. In 2013, he was sent off at 7/1 in the _RSA Chase_, and despite a number of mistakes at his fences, he managed to clinch a third place dividend for each way backers. The following year, _Nicky Henderson_ entered **Hadrian's Approach** in the _Baylis & Harding Affordable Luxury Handicap Chase_, and despite being second favourite for the race at a price of 8/1, the bay gelding never troubled the leaders and came home well beaten in 14th.

To date, **Hadrian's Approach** is the only **High Chaparral** sired horse to have taken part in Cheltenham Festival chase events. Bar a solitary run in the 2015 _Weatherbys Champion Bumper_ by **Montana Belle**, the rest of the offspring's festival appearances have taken place over hurdles, of which a staggering 10 of 14 have taken place in the festival's novice hurdle events confined to four year olds. Four of these 4 year olds took their chance in the _JCB Triumph Hurdle_, and with starting prices of 66/1, 100/1, 150/1 and 200/1, it is easy to see why all bar one of the runners was pulled up or finished tailed off. The most encouraging run came from **Wingtips** who attained a fifth place finish in the 2012 renewal. The other six **High Chaparral** sired 4 year olds made their festival appearances in the _Fred Winter Juvenile Novices' Handicap Hurdle_, and with the odds of all six runners ranging between 25/1 and 100/1, not many punters fancied their chances. **Indian Groom** at 33/1 was the first of **High Chaparral**'s representatives to run in the _Fred Winter_, and it was a very respectable performance to finish in 5th and just half a length outside of the places. The next four runners who took part in this novices' handicap ran in accordance with market expectations, but that was not the case with the _Tim Easterby_ trained **Hawk High**, who belied his 33/1 starting price when winning the 2014 renewal, staying on strongly in the closing stages to hold off the _Paul Nicholls_ trained, _Katgary_.

Considering that 14 of the 17 **High Chaparral** bred festival runners were sent off at odds greater than 20/1, including seven runners considered rank outsiders with an SP of between 50/1 and 200/1, to have a festival record of two victories and a place is admirable. The reality is that if one had placed a £1.00 each way wager on all seventeen of the progeny's festival outings, it would have resulted in a profit of £18.45.

With so few runs on which to base any firm conclusions, a sizable chunk of caution is recommended if taking on board my advice as to the chances of **High Chaparral**'s offspring at the 2017 Cheltenham Festival. Nevertheless, for what it is worth, if you come across a festival entry sired by **High Chaparral**, that isn't a 50/1 plus outsider, and you fancy the horse's chances, then my recommendation is to place your bet and back your judgement.

Kalanisi (IRE)

Quote from the 2016 Cheltenham Festival Stallion Guide - "Should any **Kalanisi** sired horse with an SP of 14/1 or less, be entered in a two mile hurdle race at the 2016 Cheltenham Festival, then the trends suggest that the runner will finish in the first six positions and a 28% percent chance that the horse will win."

Kalanisi (21-y-o)

Race Format	Miles	Won	Placed	Unplaced	Total	Win %	Place %
	About 2m	2	2	6	10	20%	40%
Hurdles	About 2m 4f	0	0	5	5	0%	0%
	About 3m	0	0	2	2	0%	0%
	About 2m	0	0	0	0	-	-
Chases	About 2m 4f	0	0	1	1	0%	0%
	About 3m	0	0	0	0	-	-
	About 4m	0	0	0	0	-	-
Bumper	About 2m	0	0	2	2	0%	0%
Total		**2**	**2**	**16**	**20**	**10%**	**20%**

In previous Stallion Guides, I've highlighted that six of the seven **Kalanisi** sired runners who started at 14/1 or less in the festival's two mile hurdle events, finished in the top six places. With this in mind, and the fact that the offspring have achieved a 1st, 2nd and 3rd in four runs in the *Triumph Hurdle*, my advice has been to take note of fancied **Kalanisi** bred runners in two mile hurdle races and especially in the *Triumph Hurdle*. Sound recommendation maybe, but rather irrelevant in recent years, due to there being a dearth of **Kalanisi** sired entries in the festival's two mile hurdle contests!

The reality is that in the past five years, **Kalanisi's** progeny have participated in just one Cheltenham Festival 2m hurdle race, the 2014 running of the *Vincent O'Brien County Handicap Hurdle*, a race in which two of the offspring finished 9th and 10th and within a neck of each other. Bizarrely, the two horses in question, *Alaivan* (10/1) who finished in front of *Barizan* (50/1), raced against each other four years earlier in the 2010 *JCB Triumph Hurdle*. On this occasion, both horses managed to reward punters with a place dividend, with *Barizan* (14/1) finishing runner-up and seven lengths ahead of *Alaivan* (9/2), who finished third. A **Kalanisi** bred runner went one better in the *JCB Triumph Hurdle* of 2007, when *Katchit*, at odds of 11/2, won impressively by 9 lengths. At the next festival meeting, trainer *Alan King* entered *Katchit* to race in the 2008 *Smurfit Kappa Champion Hurdle Challenge Trophy*, and although not as straightforward as his *Triumph Hurdle* success, he still managed to clinch victory, staying on under pressure to beat the *David Pipe* trained *Osana* by one length. *Katchit*, incidentally, was the very first of **Kalanisi's** progeny to appear at a Cheltenham Festival, so following his two successes in 2007 and 2008, the festival statistics for **Kalanisi** bred horses at that time read 2 wins from 2 runs! **Katchit** attempted to make it 3 out of 3 for the offspring in the 2009 *Smurfit Kappa Champion Hurdle Challenge Trophy*, but at odds of 12/1, he finished sixth and some six lengths behind the 22/1 winner, *Punjabi*.

In the past 8 Cheltenham Festivals, there have been eighteen races in which **Kalanisi** sired runners have attempted to add to *Katchit's* two victories, but the closest that any of them have come was with *Barizan* and *Alaivan* in the aforementioned 2010 *JCB Triumph Hurdle*. Indeed, these are the only two place positions recorded against **Kalanisi's** stock.

At last year's festival, there were two entries from **Kalanisi**'s offspring, the first of which was *Jot'em Down*, who ran in accordance with his 100/1 starting price, when finishing 19th of 23 in the *Weatherbys Champion Bumper*. The second of the **Kalanisi** bred runners, *Barters Hill*, was to take his chance in Friday's *Albert Bartlett Novices' Hurdle*, and he was well fancied, due to him being unbeaten from winning all seven of his races to date. Trained by *Ben Pauling* and ridden by *David Bass*, the 4/1 chance, having led for much of the race, found himself under pressure heading towards the last hurdle and had no extra to give in the last 100 yards, and eventually had to settle for 4th and outside the places. To date, that 4th spot achieved by *Barters Hill*, is the highest festival placing that **Kalanisi**'s offspring have achieved outside of races within the two mile hurdle category.

In summary, punters should ignore **Kalanisi** sired runners at the 2017 Cheltenham Festival, unless they are entered in a two mile hurdle race, in which case, they are probably worth supporting. I will certainly be very interested in any of the progeny's 2m hurdle runners should the entrant's odds be 14/1 or less. As advised earlier, in previous festivals, six of the seven **Kalanisi** sired runners who had met these criteria finished in the top six places, including 2 winners and 2 places. And perhaps a 14/1 cut off point is too conservative, as no **Kalanisi** bred runner has run in a festival 2m hurdle event at odds of between 16/1 and 33/1. The shortest starting price of the three outsiders to have run in the festival's 2m hurdle races, is the 40/1 attached to *Simarian*, when he finished 7th in the 2009 *JCB Triumph Hurdle*.

So, come March, let's keep our fingers crossed that at least one **Kalanisi** bred entrant will be amongst the list of runners in the festival's two mile hurdle contests. And should the horse be reasonably well supported, a small bet would be my recommendation.

Kapgarde (FR)

Kapgarde was not featured in the 2016 Cheltenham Festival Stallion Guide.

Kapgarde (18-y-o)							
Race Format	*Miles*	*Won*	*Placed*	*Unplaced*	*Total*	*Win %*	*Place %*
	About 2m	0	1	7	8	0%	13%
Hurdles	About 2m 4f	0	1	3	4	0%	25%
	About 3m	0	0	2	2	0%	0%
	About 2m	0	0	0	0	-	-
Chases	About 2m 4f	0	0	5	5	0%	0%
	About 3m	0	0	2	2	0%	0%
	About 4m	0	0	1	1	0%	0%
Bumper	About 2m	0	0	1	1	0%	0%
Total		**0**	**2**	**21**	**23**	**0%**	**9%**

Kapgarde has not featured in previous Cheltenham Festival Stallion Guides, as until now, it has been difficult to provide any meaningful conclusions. But with five runners at the 2016 festival, the stallion's offspring have now amassed 23 runs in total, and just enough information on which to provide an initial analysis and commentary.

Based on the 23 runs to date, **Kapgarde**'s offspring have landed just two place positions at Cheltenham Festivals, so the early signs are not encouraging. The first of those placings occurred in the 2012 *Vincent O'Brien County Handicap Hurdle* when *Edgardo Sol* (25/1), ridden by *Harry Derham* claiming seven pounds, was unable to catch the winner, *Alderwood*, who was ably assisted by the vastly more experienced top jockey, *A P McCoy*.

Four years later, five **Kapgarde** sired runners made appearances at the 2016 Cheltenham Festival, one of whom, **Ubak**, at odds of 28/1, managed to secure a third place finish in the *Coral Cup*. It was the second time that the *Gary Moore* trained gelding had participated at a Cheltenham Festival. Three years before, he had finished 7th of 8 runners at odds of 100/1 in the 2013 *Neptune Investment Management Novices' Hurdle*, before winning the following month at *Aintree*, in the *John Smith's Mersey Novices' Hurdle*. Following a trip to Ireland, just under 3 weeks later, when he was second of three behind *Un Atout*, in *Punchestown's Tattersalls Ireland Champion Novice Hurdle*, he was not seen on a racecourse for 945 days. Returning at *Newbury* in November 2015 in the first of three Novice Chases, he reverted back to hurdles in the *Totepool National Spirit Hurdle* at *Fontwell* in February 2016, before his satisfying return to Cheltenham in the *Coral Cup* last spring.

The other four **Kapgarde** bred representatives at last year's festival recorded a 5th, 6th, 8th and a faller named *Garde La Victoire*, who was going well enough before falling four out in the *JLT Novices' Chase*. It is worth noting that of the 23 festival runners of **Kapgarde**'s stock, ten of them have registered finishing positions of between 5th and 9th in their respective races, so last year's results were not out of line with previous performances from the offspring.

With a 9% place strike rate and having yet to provide a winner from 23 festival runs, a £30.75 loss would have been the result if one had placed a £1.00 each way bet on all of Kapgarde's festival representatives to date. With that in mind, the only conclusion to be drawn at this time is to advise punters to be wary of placing bets on **Kapgarde** sired festival entries.

Karinga Bay (GB)

Quote from the 2016 Cheltenham Festival Stallion Guide - "The 32nd attempt by the offspring to win a festival race was going to take place in Friday's showpiece event – the *Betfred Cheltenham Gold Cup Chase*. The stallion's representative in the race was a horse called *Coneygree*, who had won seven of his nine races under rules."

Karinga Bay (Died as a 20-y-o in 2006)							
Race Format	*Miles*	*Won*	*Placed*	*Unplaced*	*Total*	*Win %*	*Place %*
	About 2m	0	0	2	2	0%	0%
Hurdles	About 2m 4f	0	0	5	5	0%	0%
	About 3m	0	1	3	4	0%	25%
	About 2m	0	0	0	0	-	-
Chases	About 2m 4f	0	0	5	5	0%	0%
	About 3m	1	2	2	5	20%	60%
	About 4m	0	0	1	1	0%	0%
Bumper	About 2m	0	0	0	0	-	-
Total		**1**	**3**	**18**	**22**	**5%**	**18%**

In last year's Guide, I highlighted the fact that **Karinga Bay**'s remaining progeny were now in their later years and, as a result, any of the offspring that were high enough in the National Hunt Official Ratings to go to Cheltenham, would most likely be running in longer distance chase events at the festival. I also advised that the category where **Karinga Bay** sired runners had enjoyed most success was in three mile chases with two places and one win from a total of just five runs.

The clue to who is responsible for that 3m chase victory, which is in fact the one and only festival success across all race categories to be recorded by **Karinga Bay**'s progeny, is highlighted in the quote at the top of the page. Having triumphed in the 2015 *Betfred Cheltenham Gold Cup Chase*, it was a huge shame that trainer *Mark Bradstock*'s plan for **Coneygree** to defend his crown the following season was derailed in December 2015, when his stable star was ruled out for the remainder of the season due to slab fractures in both hocks. It is hoped that **Coneygree** will race in the 2017 *Timico Cheltenham Gold Cup Chase*, although at the time of writing, this is also open to doubt. He missed the *32Red King George VI Chase* at *Kempton* on Boxing Day after failing to show his usual sparkle and has since been found to have jarred himself up. He is clearly a fragile sort having run just twice since his 2015 *Gold Cup* victory, but it was the same story before he won Cheltenham's showpiece event. His first ever victory over fences occurred on 28th November 2014 when he overcame a 671-day absence from the racecourse after picking up an injury ahead of the 2013 Cheltenham Festival. Earlier that month, his comeback had originally been intended to take place at *Plumpton*, but a vet controversially insisted that **Coneygree** was lame and so the horse had to be withdrawn. **Coneygree** has had a number of wind operations and a range of other niggles, none of which stopped him before.

I really hope **Coneygree** makes it to Cheltenham, as if he doesn't show, there is a reasonable chance that **Karinga Bay**'s progeny will be unrepresented at the festival. The reality is that the youngest of the offspring will be ten years old this year, and apart from **Coneygree**'s triumphant run, the only other **Karinga Bay** sired festival runner in the past two years has been the *Charlie Longsdon* trained, **Killala Quay**. In 2015, at odds of 11/1, **Killala Quay** was pulled up before two out in the *CHAPS*

Restaurants Barbados Novices' Handicap Chase, over a distance of 2m4½f. Last year, he attempted the same race again, albeit under a new sponsor, and fared little better, this time finishing 14th of 20 runners in the *Close Brothers Novices' Handicap Chase*. **Karinga Bay**'s progeny have had five attempts in 2½ mile festival chases in the past decade, and last year's 14th from *Killala Quay* was unusual only on the basis that on the other four occasions, **Karinga Bay**'s representatives were all pulled up!

The offspring's runners have performed much better in 3m chases, where in a total of five festival races, the **Karinga Bay** bred entries have all finished in the first eight places. In addition to *Coneygree*'s Gold Cup victory, two place dividends have been recorded by *Our Mick*, who achieved both his place positions in the *JLT Specialty Handicap Chase*, finishing third in 2012 at 11/1 and going one better the following year when finishing runner-up as the 13/2 favourite. The two unplaced efforts, by **Karinga Bay** sired runners, occurred in the *Foxhunter Chase Challenge Cup*. *Bradley*, at 25/1, put up a reasonable show in finishing 8th in 2012 and two years later, 5/1 favourite, *Harbour Court* finished up the field in fifth place.

Looking ahead to the 2017 Cheltenham Festival, I will take account of any **Karinga Bay** bred entries in three mile chase events, and that includes *Coneygree*, should he make it to this year's *Timico Cheltenham Gold Cup Chase*. Outside of this race category, the offspring can be safely ignored having achieved just four top six positions in 28 attempts.

Kayf Tara (GB)

Quote from the 2016 Cheltenham Festival Stallion Guide - "If we disregard *The Package* and *Alfie Sherrin* from the statistics, then from 60 runners, **Kayf Tara**'s progeny have recorded just five place dividends and a solitary victory which was achieved in the 2009 *Pertemps Final*, by the *Venetia Williams* trained, *Kayf Aramis*. This amounts to a 10% win and place strike rate and a rather miserable win strike rate of less than 2%. Betting on **Kayf Tara**'s progeny at Cheltenham Festivals is not for me."

	**Kayf Tara (23-y-o)**
Race Format	*Miles*	*Won*	*Placed*	*Unplaced*	*Total*	*Win %*	*Place %*
	About 2m	0	0	9	9	0%	0%
Hurdles	About 2m 4f	0	2	15	17	0%	12%
	About 3m	2	1	15	18	11%	17%
	About 2m	0	3	8	11	0%	27%
Chases	About 2m 4f	0	0	9	9	0%	0%
	About 3m	3	4	14	21	14%	33%
	About 4m	0	0	4	4	0%	0%
Bumper	About 2m	1	0	4	5	20%	20%
Total		6	10	78	94	6%	17%

The stallion, whose stock recorded the most wins at the 2016 Cheltenham Festival, was **Kayf Tara**, registering three victories. These three victories, recorded in a single year, doubled the number of wins that **Kayf Tara**'s offspring had achieved in the previous decade of festival races. 2016 was, by far, the most successful Cheltenham Festival for **Kayf Tara**'s progeny. Now look at the quote at the top of this page taken from the 2016 Cheltenham Festival Stallion Guide. "Betting on **Kayf Tara**'s progeny at Cheltenham Festivals is not for me." So how do I get out of this one? Read on!

The most obvious starting point is to calculate the profit that punters would have received at the 2016 festival had they supported **Kayf Tara** bred runners. I can reveal that if one had backed all 25 of **Kayf Tara**'s festival entries last season, it would have resulted in a loss of £8.00 to a £1.00 win stake, and for each way backers, a loss of £23.00 to a £1.00 each way stake. So perhaps striking a line through the **Kayf Tara** sired runners last year, wasn't so costly after all!

My biggest mistake, without any doubt at all, was opposing *Thistlecrack*. He is bold, powerful, intelligent, and the way he wins his races is effortless. He is a very impressive horse and oozes quality. The only slight chink in his armoury is probably the fact that he can be a little too exuberant. In hindsight, the fact that I opposed him can only be put down to a moment of madness! Before his facile victory in last season's *Ryanair World Hurdle*, I was concerned that the only time he had raced on good going was in his second ever race, a National Hunt Flat Race at *Wincanton* in April 2014. Although, once again, I'm unsure as to why I was worried. He won easily! My other issue was that he was out of **Kayf Tara**, whose offspring's record at Cheltenham Festivals was a 4% win strike rate.

At the tail end of 2016, having been impressive in winning three novice chases at *Chepstow*, *Cheltenham* and *Newbury*, he was installed as the favourite for the 2017 *Timico Cheltenham Gold Cup Steeple Chase*. Then, on Boxing Day at *Kempton Park*, he annihilated stablemate *Cue Card* and three other rivals to win the *32Red King George VI Chase*, a performance so awe-inspiring that his

Gold Cup odds were slashed to odds-on. It would be a wonderful story if, following the disappointment of *Cue Card*'s fall in the 2016 *Gold Cup*, Colin Tizzard's other stable star, **Thistlecrack**, could win the big one come March. For sure, it won't be easy for this novice chaser to win the big prize. We should remember that before *Coneygree*'s victory in the 2015 *Betfred Cheltenham Gold Cup*, the last time that a novice won a *Gold Cup* was when *Captain Christy*, ridden by *Bobby Beasley*, triumphed in 1974. My personal view is that if *Coneygree* can win the *Gold Cup* after just three races over fences, then I'm sure that **Thistlecrack** can do the same. That said, as history shows, it is a very hard race for a novice to win.

Although **Kayf Tara**'s progeny have a relatively low win strike-rate of just over 6%, we should be cognizant of the fact that **Kayf Tara** is very capable of producing the odd extraordinary racehorse that performs well at Cheltenham Festivals. In last year's Guide, I pointed out that just two of **Kayf Tara**'s offspring, **The Package** and **Alfie Sherrin**, were responsible for all of the win and place positions that the progeny had achieved in the festival's 3m chase category. There aren't too many twelve year old horses who are victorious at Cheltenham Festivals, so when **The Package** lined up, himself a 12 year old, at the start of the 2015 *Fulke Walwyn Kim Muir Challenge Cup Handicap Chase*, some of us may have thought that this would be one race too many for him. But **The Package** proved that if you are an exceptional horse, then age is no barrier, and the *David Pipe* gelding romped home, ridden by that exceptional amateur rider, *Jamie Codd*. Even though I had not backed the winner, I was delighted that **The Package**, owned by the family of the late *David Johnson*, had finally won a race at a Cheltenham Festival. He fully deserved the victory, having picked up three place dividends previously, and all in the same race, albeit with different sponsors. In 2010, he missed out by a head to finish runner-up to *Chief Dan George* in the *William Hill Trophy Handicap Chase*. Two years later, he finished fourth to **Alfie Sherrin** in the *JLT Specialty Handicap Chase* and then in 2014, as an 11 year old, he finished third in the *Baylis & Harding Affordable Luxury Handicap Chase*. In terms of Cheltenham Festival wins and places, **The Package** has been the most successful of **Kayf Tara**'s offspring, albeit his haul of £66.715.50 in festival prize money was achieved in handicap events, hence dwarfed by **Thistlecrack**'s £170,850 that was secured by winning last year's *Ryanair World Hurdle*.

Before last season, out of 70 festival runs, the three victories from **Kayf Tara** bred runners were all achieved in handicap races, so the 2016 Cheltenham Festival was quite a turnaround for the stallion, where we witnessed not only a doubling of wins, but all three of them were attained in prestigious non-handicap Grade 1 races. I have always thought that you need a tough horse with stamina reserves to win the *RSA Chase*, and so it proved last year, when the *Nigel Twiston-Davies* trained, **Blaklion**, stayed on gamely to win the 2016 renewal by ½ length from *Shaneshill*. It was a hugely exciting race, with the front four all in with a chance when jumping the final fence, but it was the **Kayf Tara** sired, **Blaklion**, who was the strongest of the quartet up the final, punishing hill. The race took its toll on the 3rd and 4th home. *More Of That*, the 6/4 favourite, who finished 3rd, broke blood vessels in the latter stages of the race, whilst *No More Heroes* faded into 4th after he struck into himself on his left fore and suffered a severed tendon. Sadly, the injury proved to be so severe that later that evening, *Giggingstown House Stud* made the decision to put the horse down.

So having trained the very first Cheltenham Festival Grade 1 victory for **Kayf Tara** sired horses in the *RSA Chase*, we had to wait little more than three hours, for *Nigel Twiston-Davies* to do the same again, and provide us with the second Grade 1 winner for the progeny, in the *Weatherbys Champion Bumper*. **Ballyandy** returned the 5/1 second favourite, but it needed a photo to confirm that he had beaten the *Willie Mullins* trained *Battleford* (25/1) by just a nose. In winning the race, **Ballyandy** stands alone as being the only **Kayf Tara** sired horse to win a Cheltenham Festival race at a distance other than three miles.

Based on three victories at last year's Cheltenham Festival, plus the one place position, attained by *Special Tiara*'s 3rd in the *Betway Queen Mother Champion Chase*, perhaps my conclusions surrounding **Kayf Tara** should be re-evaluated. Or perhaps not, as the numbers in the table above, based upon the past ten years, are unambiguous in highlighting a win strike rate of just 6% and a win and place strike rate of 17%. Interestingly, with 25 runners from **Kayf Tara**'s offspring at last year's Cheltenham Festival, the three wins and one place resulted in the win and place strike being unchanged from the previous season, at 17%. And although the festival win strike rate has jumped over the past 12 months from 4% to 6%, the fact remains that supporting **Kayf Tara**'s stock at the festival is unprofitable. Even in the most successful year for the stallion, when the progeny recorded more victories than any other sire's brood, anyone who had backed all of **Kayf Tara**'s offspring at last year's Cheltenham Festival would have still made a loss.

In summary, I regard *Thistlecrack* as an exceptional racehorse, and there is a definite possibility that he will achieve even greater success for his connections, and in so doing, may even improve the Cheltenham Festival statistics for **Kayf Tara**'s stock. However, if one takes *Thistlecrack* out of the picture, than I am of the opinion that the 2016 Cheltenham Festival will be as good as it gets for **Kayf Tara**, where the progeny secured a victory for one in every 8 runs. Over the past decade, the festival win strike rate is 6%, not last year's 12%, and that equates to losing 15 bets before finding a winner, which in turn means losses rather than profits. For **Kayf Tara** bred runners at the 2017 Cheltenham Festival, by all means, bet on *Thistlecrack*. As for the rest, strike a line through them.

King's Theatre (IRE)

Quote from the 2016 Cheltenham Festival Stallion Guide - "Punters may be interested to learn that at the last ten Cheltenham Festivals, 23 of the 102 King's Theatre sired runners have lined up at odds of 6/1 or shorter of which 10 have won, which is a very healthy 43% win strike rate. Backing these 23 shorter priced runners, rather than all 102 of the progeny, would have delivered a larger profit of £29.88 to a £1.00 win stake."

King's Theatre (Died as a 20-y-o in 2011)

Race Format	Miles	Won	Placed	Unplaced	Total	Win %	Place %
	About 2m	1	3	10	14	7%	29%
Hurdles	About 2m 4f	3	2	19	24	13%	21%
	About 3m	3	3	9	15	20%	40%
	About 2m	1	2	5	8	13%	38%
Chases	About 2m 4f	2	2	12	16	13%	25%
	About 3m	2	2	23	27	7%	15%
	About 4m	2	0	6	8	25%	25%
Bumper	About 2m	1	2	7	10	10%	30%
Total		**15**	**16**	**91**	**122**	**12%**	**25%**

At the last 10 Cheltenham Festivals, 74 of King's Theatre's progeny have registered 122 runs between them. The most familiar names sired by King's Theatre who have won at the festival are *Captain Chris, Menorah, Riverside Theatre, The New One, Wichita Lineman, Balthazar King* and of course, *Cue Card*, who is probably the most renowned and popular of all of King's Theatre's offspring.

Trained by Dorset based *Colin Tizzard*, *Cue Card* has won twice at the Festival, securing victory in the 2013 *Ryanair Chase* three years after his 40/1 trouncing of the opposition in the 2010 *Weatherbys Champion Bumper*. Last season, *Cue Card* returned to the Cheltenham Festival once again in an effort to win the *Cheltenham Gold Cup*, and in so doing, earn a £1m bonus for connections by completing the Jockey Club Racecourses new Chase Triple Crown that was launched in the autumn of 2015. A recent wind operation had played a part in *Cue Card's* performances last season and had no doubt helped him to secure the first two legs of the Chase Triple Crown, winning the *Betfair Chase* at *Haydock* and *Kempton Park's King George VI Chase*. In the *Timico Cheltenham Gold Cup Chase*, the fairy tale didn't materialise, as *Cue Card* barely took off at the 3rd last fence and fell horribly. To the delight of the crowd, however, he quickly leapt up to his feet. At the time of his fall, he was travelling well and disputing the lead, but personally, I still don't believe he would have beaten the eventual winner, *Don Cossack*. It had been the first time that *Cue Card* had been back at the festival since his victory in the 2013 *Ryanair Chase*. He was ruled out of running in 2014 after pulling muscles in his back and twelve months later, he missed the festival again due to a small wind problem.

Cue Card was one of 24 of King's Theatre's progeny to run at the 2016 Cheltenham Festival, and lining up at odds of 5/2, he was one of just 3 of the 24 to have a starting price of 6/1 or less. I mention this, as in last year's Guide, I advised punters that when it came to King's Theatre, a profitable policy was to back any King's Theatre sired runner whose odds are 6/1 or less, a strategy which before last season's festival would have provided a profit of £29.88 to a £1.00 win stake. Of the other two shorter priced **King's Theatre** bred runners last year, *The New One* (7/2), trained by *Nigel Twiston-Davies*, finished a well beaten 4th in the *Stan James Champion Hurdle Challenge Trophy* and *Balthazar King* (9/2) fell at around half way in the *Glenfarclas Cross Country Chase*. In *Balthazar King*'s case, horse, trainer (*Philip Hobbs*) and jockey (*Richard Johnson*) were going for a hat-trick of wins in the *Glenfarclas Chase* as the combination had already won the event in their previous two attempts at the race in 2012 and 2014. However, it wasn't to be.

Despite the fact that *Cue Card*, *The New One* and *Balthazar King* failed to add to the victories for **King's Theatre**'s offspring at last season's festival, I would still advise punters not to abandon the "back any **King's Theatre** sired runner whose odds are 6/1 or less" strategy. As it stands today, over the past ten Cheltenham Festivals, 26 of the 122 **King's Theatre** sired runners have raced at odds of 6/1 or shorter, and ten of them won, which is a very healthy 38% win strike rate. Backing these 26 shorter priced runners would have delivered a profit of £26.88 to a £1.00 win stake.

In hurdle events at the festival, the best results for **King's Theatre**'s stock are in the three mile category where the progeny have delivered a 20% win strike rate. In the *Albert Bartlett Novices' Hurdle (registered as the Spa Novices' Hurdle)*, there have been 8 runs by **King's Theatre**'s offspring, resulting in two victories (*Wichita Lineman* in 2007 and *Brindisi Breeze* in 2012). Of the other six to have run, four of them started at 50/1 or bigger and unsurprisingly they all finished down the field, although that may be unkind to *The Druids Nephew* who at 100/1 finished 6th and some 18 lengths behind *Brindisi Breeze* in the 2012 running. The two remaining contenders were both at much shorter prices, with *African Gold* (9/2) finishing 2nd to *At Fishers Cross* in the 2013 event and the *David Pipe* trained *Kings Palace* (5/2) falling when well beaten in 2014.

In the 3m handicap hurdle event at the festival, the *Pertemps Network Final*, the two **King's Theatre**'s offspring who took part in the 2015 running, *Junction Fourteen* (33/1) and *Regal Encore* (15/2 favourite), both failed to finish in the top six positions. It was a different story, the year before however, where followers of the progeny were rewarded with the winner and runner-up. In an exciting finish, the 9/2 favourite, *Fingal Bay* just managed to out battle *Southfield Theatre* at 20/1 to win by a nose, which delivered a Tote Exacta Forecast dividend of £121.20. The only other horse from **King's Theatre**'s stock to have run in the *Pertemps Final* was in 2012 when *Palace Jester* at 66/1 made all the running until fading between the last two hurdles and finishing down the field in 12th. The progeny have only ever had two runners in the 3m *Ladbrokes World Hurdle*, *Wichita Lineman* finishing down the field in 2008 and *Voler La Vedette* (20/1) finishing second and giving *Big Buck's* a huge fright in the 2012 running.

It was a shame that there weren't any runners from **King's Theatre**'s stock in last year's 3m hurdle races, as based upon a 40% win and place strike rate over the past decade, the progeny typically perform well in these festival events.

In the two mile hurdle category, in the six Cheltenham Festivals between 2010 and 2015, **King's Theatre**'s progeny has been represented on 4 occasions in the *Supreme Novices Hurdle* and on 3 occasions in the *Champion Hurdle*. In those seven runs in total, all of the **King's Theatre** bred runners finished in the first five positions, including one winner, *Menorah* (12/1) who was victorious in the 2010 *Supreme Novices Hurdle*. Last season, *The New One* continued the pattern by finishing 4th in the *Stan James Champion Hurdle Challenge Trophy*. Unfortunately, in the festival's traditional opening event, *Bellshill* at 11/1, albeit the second string of the three *Willie Mullins*' trained runners in the race, rather let the side down and broke the trend, finishing 13th and second last in the 2016 *Sky Bet Supreme Novices' Hurdle*. With **King's Theatre**'s progeny, having achieved a top 5 position in 8 out of 9 attempts in the aforementioned Grade 1 hurdle events over the past seven years, punters may be tempted to think that backing the progeny in these races would be highly rewarding. I would advise caution, however, as the reality is that the profit has been negligible and rather reliant upon the fact that the solitary victory was achieved with the biggest starting price of all of the nine runners, that being *Menorah*'s 12/1 success as previously mentioned. Of the other 8 appearances, there have been two place positions, these being *Shaneshill* at 9/1 who was runner-up to stablemate, *Douvan*, in the 2015 *Sky Bet Supreme Novices' Hurdle*, thereby providing a 1-2 for trainer *Willie Mullins*, and *The New One*, who finished 3rd in the 2014 *Stan James Champion Hurdle Challenge Trophy*. For the record, backing all nine of *King's Theatre*'s bred runners in these two races over the past decade would have delivered a profit of £4.00 to a £1.00 win stake or £2.87 to a £1.00 each way stake.

The only other Cheltenham Festival two mile hurdle event that *King's Theatre*'s bred runners have contested in the past decade is the Grade 3 *Vincent O'Brien County Handicap Hurdle*, and previous to last year, the four attempts in the race had failed to deliver a top five finish. That said, with odds of 12/1, 20/1, 33/1 and 66/1, we shouldn't be surprised. *Fethard Player*, owned and trained by *Billy Treacy*, was the *King's Theatre* sired runner in the 2016 *Vincent O'Brien County Handicap Hurdle*, and with a starting price of 33/1, one could be forgiven for expecting another 'also-ran' performance from the progeny. But *Fethard Player* bucked the trend, staying on well to finish runner-up and two and a half lengths behind the *Dan Skelton* trained *Superb Story*.

If *Fethard Player*'s performance was somewhat unanticipated, then the same could be said for *Diamond King*'s victory in the *Coral Cup* within the festival's 2½m hurdle category. *Davy Russell* gave the *Gordon Elliott* trained 12/1 shot a perfect ride, comfortably going into the lead approaching the last and putting the race to bed to win by 1¼ lengths from *Long House Hall*. *King's Theatre*'s offspring have run in seven Cheltenham Festival 2½m handicap hurdles since 2006 with the highest position being 9th in the 2014 running of the *Martin Pipe Conditional Jockeys' Handicap Hurdle*. We have to go back to 2005 to find a *King's Theatre* sired horse doing better in a 2½m handicap hurdle and it occurred in the 2005 *Coral Cup*, where two of the offspring were entered. Of the pair, it was the *Tom Taaffe* trained *Tumbling Dice* (16/1) who performed best, securing third place, and some seven lengths ahead of the other *King's Theatre* sired runner, *Fountain Hill* (12/1), who finished eighth.

Perhaps *Diamond King* is the precursor of better things to come for the progeny in the festival's 2½ mile handicap hurdle events, but until I see further evidence, I will stick with looking out for *King's Theatre*'s stock in the 2½ mile hurdle events that are non-handicaps, specifically the Grade 1 OLBG *Mares' Hurdle*, where the offspring have performed rather well in my opinion. The most successful of the *King's Theatre* sired mares to have taken part in this race, is the *Willie Mullins* trained, *Glens Melody*. Having finished runner-up to prolific stablemate, *Quevega*, in 2014, *Glens Melody* went one better the following year, when benefitting from the infamous last flight fall of *Annie Power*, who was yet another *W P Mullins* trained odds-on favourite. At the line, it was a close run thing, but jockey *Paul Townend* pushed out the 6/1 second favourite all out to the line, to claim victory by just a head from runner-up, *Polly Peachum*, who came home a neck in front of the third home, *Bitofapuzzle*. In the nine races of this mares' hurdle event, the first of which took place at the 2008 Cheltenham Festival, *King's Theatre*'s progeny have been represented on no less than fifteen occasions, and five of the six runners who lined up at odds of 25/1 or less finished in the first five places. Considering the fact that *Quevega* monopolised this specific race by winning six of the nine contests to date, the performances of *King's Theatre* bred runners in this event are encouraging. The remaining nine of *King's Theatre* sired runners who took part in this event started at odds ranging from 33/1 to 200/1 and with the exception of *Stephanie Kate* (50/1) who finished fifth in the 2011 *David Nicholson Mares' Hurdle*, all of them finished well down the field. As we are on the topic of 2½ non-handicap festival hurdle events, I must also highlight the one and only appearance by a *King's Theatre* bred horse in the *Neptune Investment Management Novices' Hurdle* which resulted in a triumph for the *Twiston-Davies* family. The year was 2013, when **The New One** (7/2), ridden by *Sam Twiston-Davies* and trained by his father, *Nigel*, took the lead approaching the last hurdle and ran on strongly to win by 4 lengths from *Rule The World*, last year's *Crabbie's Grand National Chase* winner. In my view, the statistical evidence is persuasive enough for me to advise punters to keep an eye on **King's Theatre** bred runners who take part in the any of Cheltenham's 2½m non-handicap hurdles.

Over the bigger obstacles, if we take the two mile chases, **King's Theatre**'s stock have had eight runs at Cheltenham Festivals, with five of them taking place in the *Arkle*. In 2010, **Riverside Theatre** finished fifth. The following year, the *Philip Hobbs'* trained **Captain Chris** at 6/1 finished strongly to win from *Finian's Rainbow*. In 2012, the incredibly impressive *Sprinter Sacre* was in no danger of being beaten, but it was the two **King's Theatre** sired runners who filled 2nd and 3rd spot with **Cue Card** and **Menorah** respectively. *Nicky Henderson* had another "sure thing" in 2013 with *Simonsig*, who like *Sprinter Sacre* started at odds-on. Although he blundered at the 9th, he went on to win the race from another **King's Theatre** progeny in the 33/1 shot **Baily Green**. So, in that four year period of *Arkle* renewals between 2010 and 2013, we have witnessed **King's Theatre** offspring with very impressive finishing positions of first, runner-up twice, third and fifth. Last year marked the third year in a row for **King's Theatre**'s stock being unrepresented in the *Arkle*, but if the progeny do have a runner in the 2017 running, then the trends suggest we should take note.

In the middle distance chase events, **King's Theatre**'s stock was well represented at the 2016 Cheltenham Festival with six runners, four of whom took part in the 2m5f *Brown Advisory & Merriebelle Stable Plate*. Of the four, it was the *David Pipe* trained, **Kings Palace**, who performed best of the quartet, securing third place at odds of 11/1. The *JLT Novices' Chase (Registered as the Golden Miller Novices' Chase)* was established in 2011 and **L'Ami Serge** became the first of **King's Theatre**'s progeny to appear in the race. Despite a couple of jumping errors, the *Nicky Henderson* trained 8/1 shot, ridden by *Nico De Boinville*, put in a good performance in finishing third and four lengths behind winner, *Black Hercules*, one of the 4/1 co-favourites. With the last of the six runners being pulled up in the *Close Brothers Novices' Handicap Chase*, it meant that the offspring were absent from the 2½m chase of which I am most interested, the *Ryanair Chase (Registered as the Festival Trophy Chase)*. This Grade 1 race, run over a distance of two miles and five furlongs, is where **King's Theatre**'s progeny have been most successful enjoying two victories and two fourth placed positions from just six attempts in the race. The victories were courtesy of **Riverside Theatre** in 2012 and **Cue Card** in 2013, both winning at odds of 7/2. Finishing behind both victors in 4th place were two more **King's Theatre** sired runners with **Captain Chris** finishing 4th in 2012, and then in 2013, **Riverside Theatre** finishing in the same position when trying to follow-up his success of the previous season. It was **Menorah**, when past his best in the 2013 and 2014 *Ryanair* renewals, that was responsible for the two down the field runs. He was pulled up in 2013 and finished last of the ten finishers in 2014.

The statistics in the table inform us that the least impressive set of results for **King's Theatre**'s stock are in the three mile chase category. The 7% win strike rate and 15% win and place strike rate are the lowest within the seven race categories. In examining the data in detail, however, there is a clear correlation between results and starting price. Of the 27 three mile chase festival runs from the progeny within the past decade, eight of the runners started at an SP of 25/1 or bigger. Unsurprisingly, they all failed to trouble the judge, with even the highest placed runner, **Carlingford Lough** (25/1), coming home more than 20 lengths behind *Don Cossack* in finishing 4th in last year's *Timico Cheltenham Gold Cup Chase*. One may expect better from the 13 runners who lined up at odds of between 12/1 and 20/1, but they fared little better. The best performance occurred last year when **Shaneshill** at 16/1, finished behind *Blaklion* and just a ½ length away from winning the *Grade 1 RSA Chase*. In the preceding years, the highest position achieved was courtesy of **King Fontaine** finishing more than 30 lengths behind the winner, yet securing 5th spot, in the 2011 *Stewart Family*

Spinal Research Handicap Chase. So, what happened to the **King's Theatre** bred runners who were towards the head of the betting market at single figure odds? Well, two of them secured victory in the 3m event originally known as the *National Hunt Handicap Chase*, and which since the early 1980s, has had no less than seven sponsors. The first of the progeny's two successes in this race was clinched by the *Jonjo O'Neill* trained **Wichita Lineman** (5/1 Favourite) in the 2009 *William Hill Trophy Handicap Chase*, but it was a very close thing with a typically strong driving finish by *AP McCoy* in the dying strides to just get up and beat the *Daryl Jacob* ridden *Maljimar* by a neck. Six years later, this time the race being named the *Ultima Business Solutions Handicap Chase*, the victor was **The Druids Nephew**, trained by *Neil Mulholland*. Based on his previous two festival runs, where he had finished sixth on both occasions, many punters were aware that the Cheltenham Festival course held no fears for **The Druids Nephew**, and so it proved as *Barry Geraghty* rode him to a relatively comfortable victory at odds of 8/1. Just in case some of you are thinking about putting your mortgage on any **King's Theatre** sired horse that takes his chance in this event, be aware that the progeny have had a total of 11 representatives in this race, and the nine who were not at the front of the market could best be described as 'also rans'. The *RSA Chase* has featured three **King's Theatre** bred runners with odds of between 4/1 and 7/1, two of whom ran in the 2015 renewal in which **Southfield Theatre** took the runner-up spot well ahead of **Kings Palace** who finished sixth, the same position that was occupied by **Carlingford Lough** in the 2014 *RSA Chase*. The only other horse that has ran at single figure odds for the offspring in the festival's 3m chases is **Cue Card**, who as was covered earlier, fell in last season's *Timico Cheltenham Gold Cup Chase*.

In the 4m category, it would be foolhardy to make any strong conclusions. With five runs on the board in the *National Hunt Chase*, **Perfect Gentleman** (10/1) has been the top performer to date, finishing fourth in the 2015 renewal. In the *Glenfarclas Cross Country Handicap Chase*, **Balthazar King** is the offspring's only representative to have run in this unique race, winning twice in 2012 and 2014, before falling last year in his bid to make it three wins out of three. A few weeks later, the dual Cheltenham Festival winner and runner-up in the 2014 *Crabbie's Grand National* was retired.

Finally, I should provide a brief comment on the chances of the progeny in the 2017 *Weatherbys Champion Bumper*. Certainly, I would not dissuade punters who want to back a **King's Theatre** sired runner in Wednesday's National Hunt Flat Race. In the past decade, the offspring have recorded a 30% win and place strike rate in this event with two runner-up performances in 2013 and 2014, following on from **Cue Card**'s 40/1 runaway victory at the 2010 Cheltenham Festival.

In each of the past three Cheltenham Festivals, more than twenty **King's Theatre** bred horses have taken part, totalling 66 runners over the past 3 years. So, come the 2017 Cheltenham Festival, and based upon the past decade of trends, we can expect the progeny's 20 or more runners to provide us with a win or place for 1 in every 4 races and a win for 1 in every 8 races. One may consider backing every **King's Theatre** sired horse that runs at the 2017 festival, a strategy which over the past 10 years would have delivered a total profit of £14.88 to a £1.00 win stake. This profit, however, is largely due to **Cue Card's** 40/1 success in the 2010 *Weatherbys Champion Bumper*. Indeed, adopting this approach over the past 4 years would have resulted in a loss every year and we need to go back to 2012 to find the last time a profit was made, when three victories from the 16 **King's Theatre** bred runners would have recorded a profit of £3.00 to a £1.00 win stake. A more selective method is needed and my overall recommendation, as previously advised, is for punters to support the progeny where the runner's odds are 6/1 or less.

If we want to delve deeper into the results, then there are a few specific races and formats, highlighted earlier and summarised below, where historically, the offspring appear to have performed better, the *Weatherbys Champion Bumper*, for instance, where **King's Theatre**'s progeny have recorded a 30% win and place strike rate. In the festival's hurdle races, I will pay particular attention to the *Sky Bet Supreme Novices' Hurdle*, the *Stan James Champion Hurdle Challenge Trophy*, non-handicaps in the 2½ mile hurdle category and all hurdle races over a distance of three miles. Over the larger obstacles, just two races for the offspring stand out for me, these being Wednesday's *Racing Post Arkle Challenge Trophy Steeple Chase* and the *Ryanair Chase* which takes place on Thursday.

Midnight Legend (GB)

Quote from the 2016 Cheltenham Festival Stallion Guide - "The finishing positions from this stallion reveal that almost half (17 of the 35 runs) have resulted in a top six finish, and of those 17 runs, eight of the horses had a starting price of 25/1 or greater. It is because of these big prices, that I highlighted how profitable it had been to back **Midnight Legend**'s offspring in each way bets at the Cheltenham Festival."

Midnight Legend (26-y-o)

Race Format	Miles	Won	Placed	Unplaced	Total	Win %	Place %
	About 2m	0	2	3	5	0%	40%
Hurdles	About 2m 4f	0	2	6	8	0%	25%
	About 3m	0	1	3	4	0%	25%
	About 2m	0	2	3	5	0%	40%
Chases	About 2m 4f	1	1	8	10	10%	20%
	About 3m	0	0	7	7	0%	0%
	About 4m	1	0	3	4	25%	25%
Bumper	About 2m	0	1	1	2	0%	50%
Total		**2**	**9**	**34**	**45**	**4%**	**24%**

I like **Midnight Legend**. And invariably, I will bet on his offspring at Cheltenham Festivals. In the quote highlighted at the top of the page, taken from last year's Guide, I advised that almost half of **Midnight Legend**'s stock to run at festival meetings attain a top six finish, and that almost half of those have a starting price of 25/1 or bigger. The one thing that can be said about **Midnight Legend**'s offspring is that they are consistent in following the trends and statistics of previous festivals. Last year, ten of the progeny took part at Cheltenham, and exactly half of them finished in the top six positions. Of the five that achieved a top six finish, four of them came home at odds of 25/1 or greater. So far so good. Last year, primarily because of the bigger odds on offer, I also advised punters how profitable it had been to back the progeny each way at Cheltenham Festivals. Unfortunately, if one had backed all ten of **Midnight Legend**'s stock that took part in the 2016 festival, the result would have been a loss of 20p to a £1.00 each way stake, so a 1% loss on stake money, despite three runner-up spots from the offspring at starting prices of 50/1, 25/1 and 9/1.

The 50/1 runner-up position was secured by *Dusky Legend*, who finished 4½ lengths behind the 8/11 favourite, *Limini*, in the festival's newest race, the *Dawn Run Mares' Novices' Hurdle*, which was sponsored by *Trull House Stud*. This hurdle race, which has expanded the festival meeting to 28 races, is run over a distance of about 2 miles and 1 furlong and is open to fillies and mares aged four years or older. *Dusky Legend* is trained by *Alan King*, who has been successful with **Midnight Legend**'s progeny at the festival before. In 2014, *Midnight Prayer* (8/1) just held on from the staying on *Shotgun Paddy* to win, by a neck, the listed 2014 *Terry Biddlecombe National Hunt Chase Amateur Riders' Novices' Chase*. And going further back, in 2007, *Robert Thornton* rode the 100/1 outsider, *Itsa Legend*, into third position in the *Brit Insurance Novices' Hurdle*.

Itsa Legend, incidentally, was the very first **Midnight Legend** bred festival runner, when he finished 8th, at 33/1, in the 2004 *Weatherbys Champion Bumper*. A decade passed before the progeny were represented for a second time in the festival's national hunt flat race, this time with 100/1 outsider, *Coyaba*, who finished 16th. Last season, at the 3rd attempt in the race, the offspring managed to reward supporters with a runner-up spot, although it was so close to being a winner. Although leading four furlongs out and running on well towards the end of the race, the *Willie Mullins* trained, *Battleford* (25/1), was eventually beaten by a nose in the final strides, by *Ballyandy*.

The third runner-up spot last year was courtesy of *Sizing John* (9/1), who finished second out of seven runners, in the *Racing Post Arkle Challenge Trophy Chase*, behind the very comfortable and odds-on winner, *Douvan*. At the previous festival, *Sizing John* had finished 3rd at odds of 25/1 in the 2015 *Sky Bet Supreme Novices' Hurdle*, which singles him out as the only one of the progeny to have delivered a win or place dividend at two Cheltenham Festivals. Put another way, the two victories and nine place positions have been achieved by ten different horses, meaning that the offspring's successes are not a reflection, say, in the dominance of just one or two horses. It should also be noted that there is no particular bias towards hurdles or fences, or indeed to any specific distance. The win and place positions of **Midnight Legend** bred runners have occurred over fences and hurdles and over distances ranging between two and four miles.

Following last season's results, of the 45 runs from the progeny over the past decade, almost half (22 of the 45 runs) have resulted in a top six finish, and of those 22 runs, twelve of the horses had a starting price of 25/1 or greater. The profit for backing all 45 of **Midnight Legend**'s offspring at £1.00 each way over the past ten Cheltenham Festivals, is £38.45 and is down to the relatively large starting prices for the win and place positions. For the record, here are those win and place results:

Itsa Legend @ 100/1 – 3rd (2007 *Brit Insurance Novices' Hurdle*)
My Petra @ 3/1 Fav – 2nd (2008 *Johnny Henderson Grand Annual Chase*)
Midnight Chase @ 100/1 – 2nd (2009 *Martin Pipe Conditional Jockeys Handicap Hurdle*)
Sparky May @ 4/1 – 2nd (2011 *David Nicholson Mares' Hurdle*)
Holmwood Legend @ 25/1 - 1st (2011 *Byrne Group Plate*)
Aimigayle @ 25/1 – 2nd (2011 *Byrne Group Plate*)
Midnight Prayer @ 8/1 – 1st (2014 *Terry Biddlecombe National Hunt Chase*)
Sizing John @ 25/1 – 3rd (2015 *Sky Bet Supreme Novices' Hurdle*)
Sizing John @ 9/1 – 2nd (2016 *Racing Post Arkle Challenge Trophy Chase*)
Battleford @ 25/1 – 2nd (2016 *Weatherbys Champion Bumper*)
Dusky Legend @ 50/1 – 2nd (2016 *Trull House Stud Mares' Novices' Hurdle*)

The 2011 *Byrne Plate* deserves further mention as no fewer than five **Midnight Legend** bred horses ran in the race, and where the two 25/1 shots, **Holmwood Legend** and **Aimigayle**, fought out the finish to secure 1st and 2nd places, resulting in a whopping tote exacta dividend of £977.70!

If you are a Cheltenham Festival devotee who likes to back a horse each way at big prices; enjoys seeing your selection up amongst the leaders; loves the smug feeling of self-satisfaction on the occasions when your big priced outsider gets placed; or feels completely elated should your selection win; then my advice is to look down the list of runners for each day of the festival, and if you happen to come across a horse that has **Midnight Legend** listed as the sire, then put your each way bet on. The trends suggest that you will get a run for your money fifty percent of the time, and for one in every four bets, you can collect some winnings.

Milan (GB)

Quote from the 2016 Cheltenham Festival Stallion Guide - "Over the past three Cheltenham Festivals, the bottom line is that **Milan** bred runners have won three and been placed on eight occasions from a total of 34 races, which translates to punters receiving a return for close to one in every three runs from the progeny. That's good enough for me."

Milan (19-y-o)							
Race Format	Miles	Won	Placed	Unplaced	Total	Win %	Place %
	About 2m	1	3	2	6	17%	67%
Hurdles	About 2m 4f	0	0	7	7	0%	0%
	About 3m	2	1	7	10	20%	30%
	About 2m	0	0	2	2	0%	0%
Chases	About 2m 4f	0	4	3	7	0%	57%
	About 3m	0	1	10	11	0%	9%
	About 4m	2	2	2	6	33%	67%
Bumper	About 2m	0	0	7	7	0%	0%
Total		**5**	**11**	**40**	**56**	**9%**	**29%**

In last year's Guide, and based upon recent performances of **Milan**'s progeny at Cheltenham Festivals, I advised that I was increasingly becoming a fan of **Milan**'s stock. My confidence was highlighted in the quote at the top of the page where, over the past three festivals, **Milan** bred runners have recorded a win or place from close to one in every three runs. At the 2016 Cheltenham Festival, this trend continued with **Milan**'s offspring attaining two victories and a 3rd place dividend from a total of nine entries. There is no doubt that from 2013 onwards, supporting **Milan**'s progeny has been highly rewarding. Backing all 43 **Milan** bred runners over the past four Cheltenham Festivals would have delivered a very welcome profit of £30.23 to a £1.00 each way stake.

The most lucrative of the Cheltenham Festival races for **Milan**'s offspring is the cross country *Glenfarclas Chase*, which until last season was a handicap but is now off level weights. Not only was *Big Shu*, at 14/1, the winner of the 2013 *Glenfarclas Handicap Chase*, he was also the very first horse sired by **Milan** to record a Cheltenham Festival victory. With the progeny's first ever festival participant, *Shadow Dancer*, finishing 20th in the 2010 *Coral Cup*, it had taken **Milan**'s stock three years to record a festival win. The following year, in 2014, *Big Shu* started as the 3/1 favourite to follow up on his success of twelve months earlier, but despite another solid performance, he was beaten by just over three lengths to finish in third. Five lengths further back, attaining a fourth place paid dividend at odds of 25/1, was the second **Milan** sired runner to take part in the race, *Duke Of Lucca*, trained by *Philip Hobbs*. *Duke of Lucca*'s second attempt to win the race in the 2015 renewal, ended in defeat, as the 5/1 shot could only finish in 8th place.

At last year's festival, I placed a rather large win bet on the 15/8 favourite, *Josies Orders* to win the *Glenfarclas Chase*. I grimaced towards the end of the race as, under *Nina Carberry*, *Josies Orders* ran on well, but not quite well enough to overtake the staying on, *Any Currency*. Over five months later, on 25th August 2016, the painful memory of my losing bet returned, when the British Horseracing Authority (BHA) announced that *Any Currency* had been disqualified from first place following a positive post-race test for the pain killer, triamcinolone acetonide. The trainer of *Any Currency*, *Martin Keighley*, was not fined by the BHA, and hence, connections were understandably saying that the trainer hadn't done anything wrong. Nevertheless, whether or not a penalty is imposed, the BHA's *Robin Mounsey* stated, "Once a horse has tested positive, the automatic consequence is that it is disqualified." The disqualification meant that *Josies Orders* was promoted to first place in the race, resulting in **Milan**'s offspring now boasting a record of two wins and two place positions from a total of five runs in the event. It is self-evident that we should be predisposed towards any **Milan** sired runner that takes part in the 2017 *Glenfarclas Cross Country Steeple Chase*.

It is interesting to note that *Josies Orders* and *Duke Of Lucca* had both previously finished down the field at the Cheltenham Festival's 3m handicap hurdle race, the *Pertemps Network Final*. Three years before his 4th place in the *Glenfarclas Chase*, *Duke of Lucca* finished 18th of 23 runners in the 2011 race, whilst in the 2014 running, *Josies Orders* finished 22nd and last of the finishers before victory in the 2016 cross-country event. Despite these two poor runs in the *Pertemps Network Final* races, Cheltenham's three mile hurdle events have been fruitful territory for other **Milan** sired entries where the progeny's strike rates within this category are 1 in 5 for a victory and 1 in 3 for a win/place. Last year, three of the nine **Milan** sired entries that participated at Cheltenham last season, ran in 3m hurdle events, two of whom lined up in the *Pertemps Network Final*. I had placed a small each way bet on the *JP McManus* owned and *Jonjo O'Neill* trained, *Join the Clan* at odds of 25/1. I was briefly excited as my selection led approaching 2 out, but *Join The Clan* had no more to give and eventually finished tenth. I had backed the wrong one. At the point where my pick had just taken the lead, approaching two from home, the other **Milan** bred runner in the race, *Mall Dini* (14/1), was starting to make headway. *Mall Dini* chased the leaders before the final hurdle, and although hanging left after jumping the last, his rider *Davy Russell*, kept him going all the way to the line, to win at odds of 14/1.

The other **Milan** sired runner to take part in a 3m hurdle event at last year's festival was *Martello Tower*, who finished seventh and well behind in the Grade 1 *Ryanair World Hurdle*. The previous season had been much more rewarding for *Martello Tower*, when he lined up in the *Albert Bartlett Novices' Hurdle*, alongside another of **Milan**'s offspring, *Milsean*. The two **Milan** bred horses fought out an exciting finish to clinch a 1st and 2nd, and with *Martello Tower* at 14/1 and *Milsean* at 33/1, supporters of **Milan**'s progeny were remunerated with a Tote Exacta Forecast dividend of £635.60. It was quite a family affair for the "*Mullins* clan" as it was the *Margaret Mullins* trained, *Martello Tower*, who just managed to out battle *Milsean*, who was ridden by her son, *Danny Mullins*, and trained by her brother-in-law, *Willie Mullins*!

With a 30% win and place strike, if one had placed a £1.00 each way bet on all ten **Milan** bred runners who had run within the festival's 3m hurdle category, a very satisfactory profit of £25.90 would have been the result. It is primarily due to the starting prices, that the returns within this category are three times greater than the profit that would have been earned had one backed all six of **Milan**'s offspring to have run in the festival's two mile hurdle events, where the stock has achieved a highly impressive 67% win and place hit rate. Indeed, the only disappointing run from the progeny has come from *Raya Star*, who finished 13th in the 2012 *Vincent O'Brien County Handicap Hurdle*. The other five **Milan** sired runners have finished in the first four, which is a highly impressive statistic. Punters should therefore take a close look at **Milan** bred runners in the festival's two mile hurdle events, albeit that we should temper our enthusiasm a smidgen as all six runners were relatively well supported in the market, with starting prices ranging from 5/1 to 9/1.

The achievements by **Milan**'s stock in hurdle events over the shortest and longest distances is in stark contrast to the results recorded within the 2½ mile category, where in seven runs to date, the highest placing is seventh. In my view, however, this is primarily explained due to the majority of **Milan** bred runners being outsiders. Three of the seven entries, for example, lined up at odds of 50/1 or greater. Similarly, if we look at the data over the bigger obstacles, punters may ponder whether to avoid **Milan**'s stock in the festival's three mile chase category, but here again, I would recommend that we look closely at the starting prices before dismissing **Milan**'s offspring out of hand. The results show just one placed effort from a total of 11 runs, but seven of the eleven runners returned an SP of 20/1 or bigger with the shortest price runner being sent off at 9/1.

To date, when it comes to the Cheltenham Festival chase events, it is only in the cross country race where **Milan**'s stock has been able to record some victories. My judgement, however, is that we won't have to wait too long before the progeny achieve a Cheltenham Festival success in the more widespread and commonplace chase events. **Milan**'s offspring have only been represented twice in 2m chase events, and as highlighted above, the poor results attained in races run at a distance of three miles, is largely explained due to the bulk of the runners being outsiders. Looking at the data in the 2½ mile chase category is perhaps the most insightful. First and foremost, **Milan** bred runners have been knocking on the door to a likely future victory, having achieved four place dividends from just a total of seven runs. And the odds of 7/1, 8/1, 10/1 and 33/1 of the four horses that managed a place position, is supportive to my rationale surrounding starting prices and their impact on the figures represented in the above table. Of the three unplaced **Milan** sired horses to have run in 2½m festival chases, two 33/1 outsiders finished well down the field and the sole 50/1 hope was our old friend, *Duke of Lucca*, who finished 5th out of ten runners in the 2012 *Jewson Novices' Chase*.

It is quite understandable for anyone to take a quick glance at the statistics table of **Milan**'s progeny and decide to support the stock in the four categories of 2m hurdles, 3m hurdles, 2½m chases and 4m chases. And in all likelihood, based on recent trends, the strategy will be rewarded with a decent profit. My assertion, however, is that there is enough evidence to suggest that **Milan** bred runners can and will perform equally as well within the other race categories, and so for me, personally, come the 2017 Cheltenham Festival, I will be very interested in supporting the progeny across the board.

Montjeu (IRE)

Quote from the 2016 Cheltenham Festival Stallion Guide - "Although **Hurricane Fly** and **Noble Prince** managed to break the "**Montjeu** bred horses don't win Cheltenham Festival races" hoodoo, the statistical evidence is convincing enough for me to put my neck on the line and predict that **Hurricane Fly**'s victory in 2013 will be the last festival victory for **Montjeu**'s offspring."

Montjeu (Died as a 16-y-o in 2012)

Race Format	Miles	Won	Placed	Unplaced	Total	Win %	Place %
	About 2m	3	4	27	34	9%	21%
Hurdles	About 2m 4f	0	0	4	4	0%	0%
	About 3m	0	0	2	2	0%	0%
	About 2m	0	0	1	1	0%	0%
	About 2m 4f	1	0	3	4	25%	25%
Chases	About 3m	0	0	2	2	0%	0%
	About 4m	0	0	0	0	-	-
Bumper	About 2m	0	0	0	0	-	-
Total		**4**	**4**	**39**	**47**	**9%**	**17%**

Let's go straight to the quote from last year's Guide where I predicted that **Hurricane Fly** would be the last **Montjeu** bred Cheltenham Festival winner. Well, at around 13.35 on Friday 18th March 2016, I was well and truly made to eat humble pie, when the **Montjeu** sired **Ivanovich Gorbatov**, romped home in the *JCB Triumph Hurdle*.

If anyone is kind enough to offer any sympathy towards me, they may wish to point out that **Ivanovich Gorbatov** was surrounded by an incredibly strong team of connections. The 9/2 favourite was officially trained by the one and only *Aidan O'Brien*, Ireland's leading Flat trainer, although it was his 22-year-old Derby winning son, *Joseph Patrick O'Brien*, who was credited with **Ivanovich Gorbatov**'s Cheltenham Festival success. The owner was none other than *J P McManus*, who since 1994, has only once, in 2011, failed to have a winner at a Cheltenham Festival. Indeed, before last year's meeting, his famous green and gold silks had been victorious at the festival on an incredible 44 occasions. Last year, *J P McManus* recorded six festival victories, although up until 25th August 2016, everyone considered he had attained five successes and hence a grand total of 49 Cheltenham Festival wins. In short, although his *Josies Orders* finished second in the 2016 *Glenfarclas Chase*, five months later, the horse was promoted to 1st place, as a result of the 'winner', *Any Currency*, being disqualified due to a positive post-race drugs test. I find it rather sad that, at the time, no one within Cheltenham's Winners Enclosure was aware that *On The Fringe*'s victory in last season's *St. James's Place Foxhunter Chase Challenge Cup*, was to be *J P McManus*'s 50th Cheltenham Festival winner.

Perhaps **Ivanovich Gorbatov** will turn out to be an exceptional racehorse, just like the most successful and renowned of **Montjeu**'s progeny, **Hurricane Fly**. But I doubt it. It was in the 2011 *Stan James Champion Hurdle Challenge Trophy*, when **Hurricane Fly** finally put an end to the statistician's cry that **Montjeu** bred horses don't win at the Cheltenham Festival. Having battled hard up the hill to beat *Peddlers Cross* by just over a length in the 2011 *Champion Hurdle*, winning as the 11/4 favourite, he was again made favourite for the following three renewals. In 2012, he started odds-on at 4/6, but could only manage third behind *Rock On Ruby*. The following season, he was to gain revenge on *Rock On Ruby* beating the *Harry Fry* trained runner by 2½ lengths to lift the

Champion Hurdle Crown for the second time. In 2014, aged ten, he tried to win the race for the third time, but on this occasion, he failed to pick up a place dividend for the first time, when finishing just outside the places in fourth. 2015 was the only year in which he didn't start as the favourite for the *Champion Hurdle*, no doubt due to the fact that he was now 11 years old. Despite his age, the *Willie Mullins* trained hurdling hero ran brilliantly to finish in third place. It was his fifth consecutive run in the race.

Five years before **Hurricane Fly** arrived on the scene, a bay gelding named **Rosecliff** was well in rear and never on terms, before being pulled up in the 2006 *Fred Winter Juvenile Novices' Handicap Hurdle*. **Rosecliff** was the very first **Montjeu** sired horse to line up in a Cheltenham Festival event, and in my view, the 15/2 shot's performance was a sign of things to come for **Montjeu's** stock, as in the main, the offspring rarely give punters a run for their money. If one takes out the five heroic performances of **Hurricane Fly**, **Montjeu** sired runners have recorded two victories and two place dividends from a total of 44 festival races. Moreover, within those 44 events, the progeny have failed to finish in the first eight positions on 29 occasions.

Montjeu's progeny tend to specialise in two mile hurdle events at the Cheltenham Festival, where within the past decade, 34 of the 47 runs have taken place. If one takes out **Hurricane Fly's** two victories and two places, the remaining **Montjeu** sired runners, alongside **Ivanovich Gorbatov's** victory, have delivered just two place positions from a total of 29 runs in the past 10 years. **Won In The Dark** finished third in the 2008 *JCB Triumph Hurdle* and the following season, **Alexander Severus** could only manage a fourth place dividend in the *Fred Winter Juvenile Novices' Handicap Hurdle*, despite being sent off as the warm 5/2 Favourite.

Over the larger obstacles, **Montjeu's** offspring have tackled the Cheltenham Festival fences on just seven occasions, and **Noble Prince's** victory in the 2011 *Jewson Novices' Chase* was rather untypical, as on the other six occasions, the offspring have all finished outside the top seven places.

Despite **Ivanovich Gorbatov** dumbfounding my sentiments last year, I cannot bring myself to change my mind about **Montjeu's** offspring. For me, the evidence is still overwhelming. When it comes to the Cheltenham Festival, my advice to punters is to avoid **Montjeu** sired runners and that includes **Ivanovich Gorbatov**, should the horse be entered at the 2017 festival. Since the bay gelding's success in the 2016 *JCB Triumph Hurdle*, at the time of writing, **Ivanovich Gorbatov** has raced over hurdles on six further occasions and hasn't won any of them.

Old Vic (GB)

Quote from the 2016 Cheltenham Festival Stallion Guide - "We should pay special attention to any **Old Vic** sired runner entered in the 2016 *Grand National*, who has previously contested a three mile race at the Cheltenham Festival."

Old Vic (Died as a 25-y-o in 2011)

Race Format	Miles	Won	Placed	Unplaced	Total	Win %	Place %
	About 2m	0	0	3	3	0%	0%
Hurdles	About 2m 4f	3	1	10	14	21%	29%
	About 3m	0	2	14	16	0%	13%
	About 2m	0	0	2	2	0%	0%
	About 2m 4f	1	4	11	16	6%	31%
Chases	About 3m	2	3	19	24	8%	21%
	About 4m	0	1	4	5	0%	20%
Bumper	About 2m	0	0	5	5	0%	0%
Total		**6**	**11**	**68**	**85**	**7%**	**20%**

This Guide is all about the Cheltenham Festival, so readers may well question why the quote at the top of this page is talking about *Aintree*'s *Grand National*. Well, when I analysed the data surrounding **Old Vic**'s success or otherwise at Cheltenham, some familiar names popped out at me from **Old Vic**'s offspring that had run well in recent *Grand Nationals*. Names like *Don't Push It*, *Comply Or Die* and *Sunnyhillboy*. So I delved deeper into the statistics to find that there was a clear correlation, which pointed to horses which had contested a 3m race at a Cheltenham Festival, very often performed well in *Grand Nationals*.

Last year, for example, who would have considered that a thirteen year old, who set off as the outsider of the entire field, would have a say in the 2016 running of the *Crabbie's Grand National Chase*. Especially, when at *Becher's Brook*, first time round, *Robbie Dunne*, the 100/1 shot's jockey, made an incredible recovery when *Vic's Canvas* pitched on landing, sending *Mr Dunne* halfway over the side and hanging off the horse's neck. And yet, somehow, the jockey managed to cling on. A few minutes later, the *Dermot Anthony McLoughlin* trained, *Vic's Canvas*, was leading the field when jumping the last, alongside eventual runner-up, *The Last Samuri*. In the end, *Vic's Canvas* weakened in the last 100 yards and eventually finished a gallant third and 14 lengths behind the winner, *Rule The World*. So, had *Vic's Canvas* contested a three mile race at Cheltenham previously? Well, just about. In the 2014 *Pertemps Network Final* run over three miles, *Vic's Canvas* lined up and was seen tracking the leaders, before falling at the very first hurdle! As well as *Vic's Canvas*, there was a second **Old Vic** bred runner in the field that met the criteria, the *Charlie Longsdon* trained *Pendra*, who completed the National course to finish in 13th at 50/1.

In finishing third, *Vic's Canvas* became the seventh of **Old Vic** sired horses to finish in the first four in the last nine *Grand Nationals*. And all seven of them had previously contested a three mile event at a Cheltenham Festival. This equates to almost 20% of the top four places being reserved for **Old Vic**'s progeny, which, for a race often described (mistakenly in my view) as a lottery, is some achievement. For the record, the other six top four *Grand National* finishers are as follows. In 2008, three years after his second in the 2005 *Royal & SunAlliance Chase*, *Comply or Die* won the *John Smith's Grand National Chase*. The following year, he ran in the *William Hill Trophy Handicap Chase* at Cheltenham, before finishing *Grand National* runner-up to the *Venetia Williams* trained 100/1 shot, *Mon Mome*.

In 2010, **Old Vic**'s offspring came up with a 1-2 at *Aintree*'s showpiece, resulting in a Tote Exacta dividend of £544.50. The winner, **Don't Push It**, who had five largely ignominious runs at the Cheltenham Festival, beat **Black Apalachi**, who finished sixth in the 2006 *Fulke Walwyn Kim Muir Handicap Chase*). **Don't Push It** finished third in the 2011 renewal and in 2012, **Sunnyhillboy** made it five years in succession for **Old Vic** offspring to record a minimum of a placed position in the event, when beaten a nose by *Neptune Collonges*. That's enough about **Old Vic** and *Aintree*. Now it's time to concentrate on my passion, the Cheltenham Festival.

Over the past decade, 55 **Old Vic** sired racehorses have registered 85 Cheltenham Festival runs between them. Of those 85 runs, six have resulted in victories and 11 have achieved a placed position. And the win and place positions are well spread-out amongst the progeny, with 14 different horses providing the 17 win and place dividends.

The three horses who have actually managed to pick up a win or place dividend at Cheltenham more than once over the past ten festivals are **Our Vic, Sunnyhillboy** and **Grand Vision**. **Grand Vision** has lined up in three festival races and has been placed twice. He finished third at the rewarding odds of 25/1 in the 2012 *Albert Bartlett Novices' Hurdle*, and in 2015, the *Colin Tizzard* trained grey was rewarded with another place dividend when finishing 4th at 11/1 in the *Fulke Walwyn Kim Muir Challenge Cup Handicap Chase*. **Our Vic,** owned by the family of the late *David Johnson*, took part in four consecutive *Festival Trophy* renewals from 2005 to 2008 inclusive. Having failed to make any sort of showing in the 2005 and 2006 contests, he finished runner-up in the 2007 event and then went one better in the same race the following year. **Sunnyhillboy**, who runs in the distinctive green-and-gold-hooped racing colours of *J P McManus*, was second in the 2010 *Byrne Group Plate*, run over 2m5f, before finally tasting victory two years later, in 2012, when winning the *Fulke Walwyn Kim Muir Challenge Cup Handicap Chase* over an extended 3m. **Sunnyhillboy** has actually run at four Cheltenham Festivals and started as the favourite on every occasion, except for his very first run, in 2009, where he finished down the field in the *Vincent O'Brien County Handicap Hurdle*. Between his placed effort and victory, he took a heavy fall in the 2011 *Stewart Family Spinal Research Handicap Chase* run over 3 miles. **Our Vic** has gone two better than **Sunnyhillboy** and has experienced a Cheltenham Festival race on six occasions. In addition to his four *Festival Trophy* runs, he recorded 3rd spot on his festival debut in the 2004 *Royal & SunAlliance Chase* and signed off his Cheltenham Festival career in 2010 when finishing down the field in the 2010 *Byrne Group Plate*.

Analysis of the results over the past ten festivals show that races within the 2½ mile category is where **Old Vic**'s progeny have been most successful. Anyone who has supported the offspring in races at this distance would have received a return in almost 1 in every 3 races. Sixteen **Old Vic** sired runners have participated in 2½ mile chase events over the past decade of Cheltenham Festivals, of which 11 have finished in the top six finishing positions. The *David Pipe* trained, **Our Vic**, stands alone as the only one of **Old Vic**'s stock to have recorded a Cheltenham Festival victory in a two and a half mile chase event, winning the 2008 *Ryanair Chase (Registered as the Festival Trophy)* at odds of 4/1. Four **Old Vic** sired runners have achieved a place dividend in 2½m festival chases, one of whom was the aforementioned **Our Vic**, who finished runner-up in the 2007 *Festival Trophy* as referenced previously. Two more of the progeny, both of whom lined up as the favourite in their respective races, finished runner-up in the *Byrne Group Plate*. **Sunnyhillboy**, as highlighted earlier, was the 6/1 favourite in the 2010 renewal and four years later, in 2014, **Colour Squadron** (5/1 favourite) had to settle for second place in the event when he finished 8 lengths behind *Ballynagour*. In the same year, **Pendra** managed to secure a place dividend by finishing 3rd at 8/1 in the *Rewards4Racing Novices' Handicap Chase*.

The best recorded win rate for **Old Vic**'s progeny over the past decade of Cheltenham Festivals is in the 2½ mile hurdles category, where **Old Vic** followers would have enjoyed three nice price successes from fourteen races. Two of those victories happened at the 2009 Cheltenham Festival. In the *Coral Cup*, **Ninetieth Minute**, ridden by *Paddy Flood* and trained by *Tom Taaffe*, provided the Irish with their seventh winner of the festival, despite it being only the second day of the meeting, when staying on strongly to secure victory at odds of 14/1. Two days later and the Irish had managed to win just two more races to record a final festival haul of nine victories. The two Irish trained representatives were out of luck in the penultimate race of the festival, the newly established *Martin Pipe Conditional Jockeys' Handicap Hurdle*, where the **Old Vic** bred, **Andytown** (25/1), won by nine lengths from the *Neil Mulholland* trained 100/1 shot, *Midnight Legend*. This conditional jockeys' race has been a rewarding race for **Old Vic** supporters, as the offspring have secured two victories and a third place from just five appearances in the event's eight runnings. In the 2012 renewal, although **Oscar Nominee** stayed on strongly towards the end of the race, he couldn't catch the two in front and eventually finished a close third at odds of 10/1. Eleven months later, the *Nicky Henderson* trained gelding was pulled up in his very next race at *Taunton*, where sadly, having been pulled up mid race, he collapsed and died. In 2015, six years after **Andytown**'s success, the *Willie Mullins* trained **Killultagh Vic** (7/1) rallied well to beat *Noble Endeavor* by a head to provide **Old Vic**'s offspring with their second victory in the event. If one had backed all fourteen **Old Vic** sired runners in the 2½m festival hurdle contests over the past 10 years, the result would have been a very rewarding £39.00 to a £1.00 each way stake.

Finally, I need to highlight the *Fulke Walwyn Kim Muir Challenge Cup Handicap Chase*. This has been a strikingly rewarding race for **Old Vic** supporters over the past five years, where the progeny have a 100% record of securing a win or place dividend. **Sunnyhillboy** started the run going when winning the event in 2012. Two years later, *Robbie McNamara* got the better of *Nina Carberry* to ride the *Jim Culloty* trained, **Spring Heeled** (12/1) to victory ahead of *Cause of Causes*. In the 2015 renewal, **Grand Vision** secured a fourth place dividend at odds of 11/1. Two more place positions were recorded for **Old Vic**'s offspring last season, when **Silvergrove** and **Knock House**, both at odds of 16/1, finished 3rd and 4th respectively behind the victor, *Cause of Causes*, who incidentally was enjoying his second successive Cheltenham Festival victory since finishing runner-up to **Spring Heeled** in 2014. So, with two victories and three places from the five **Old Vic** bred runners to have taken part in the *Kim Muir* from 2012 onwards, anyone who had backed all five representatives would have received a profit of £30.88 to a £1.00 each way stake. To complete the picture, there has only been one other **Old Vic** sired horse to take part in the *Fulke Walwyn Kim Muir Challenge Cup Handicap Chase,* this being **Black Apalachi** back in 2006, and he was hardly disgraced, finishing less than 1½ lengths out of the places in sixth.

To summarise, the trends over the past decade have pointed to big rewards being possible in supporting **Old Vic**'s progeny in the festival's 2½ mile hurdle events, especially the *Martin Pipe Conditional Jockeys' Handicap Hurdle*. Punters should also look closely at the three mile chase for amateur riders, the *Fulke Walwyn Kim Muir Challenge Cup Handicap Chase*, where the offspring have never finished out of the first six. And once the festival is over, don't forget to take a look through the 40 runners taking part at *Aintree* in the 2017 *Randox Health Grand National* to see if any **Old Vic** bred entries are amongst them who have also contested a three mile event at a Cheltenham Festival. If you find one, back it each way.

Oscar (IRE)

Quote from the 2016 Cheltenham Festival Stallion Guide - "If one had backed every **Oscar** sired runner to win at the festival from 2006 onwards, it would have resulted in a £20.30 profit to a £1 stake."

Oscar (23-y-o)

Race Format	Miles	Won	Placed	Unplaced	Total	Win %	Place %
	About 2m	1	3	9	13	8%	31%
Hurdles	About 2m 4f	2	3	14	19	11%	26%
	About 3m	2	4	23	29	7%	21%
	About 2m	1	4	5	10	10%	50%
Chases	About 2m 4f	0	0	12	12	0%	0%
	About 3m	3	4	22	29	10%	24%
	About 4m	2	0	5	7	29%	29%
Bumper	About 2m	0	0	6	6	0%	0%
Total		**11**	**18**	**96**	**125**	**9%**	**23%**

When *Barry Geraghty* lined up at the start of the 2004 *Weatherbys Champion Bumper*, I wonder if he realised that the mare underneath him, *Refinement*, was the very first of **Oscar**'s offspring to take part in a Cheltenham Festival? As it was, horse and jockey did rather well, finishing runner-up at odds of 7/1. The following year, in the 2005 *Weatherbys Champion Bumper*, *Refinement*'s trainer, *Jonjo O'Neill* entered the horse once again, ridden on this occasion by the experienced flat jockey, *Kieren Fallon*. The mare produced another fine performance, finishing 4th and 3½ lengths outside of the places, at odds of 6/1. There were two other **Oscar** sired runners in the race and both finished well done the field which wasn't a surprise in light of their 33/1 and 100/1 starting prices. This year also marked the debut of an **Oscar** sired horse tackling obstacles for the first time at a Cheltenham Festival, and at a price of 100/1, *Knock Down* didn't run too badly in finishing 7th and around 20 lengths behind the winner in the *Fulke Walwyn Kim Muir Challenge Cup Handicap Chase*.

At the 2005 Cheltenham Festival, therefore, and with SPs of 6/1, 33/1 and 100/1 twice, the outcome of no wins or places from the four **Oscar** bred runners was largely expected. Very few of us at the time, however, would have prophesied that the next 'blank' year of no wins or places for **Oscar**'s progeny would occur eleven years later at the 2016 Cheltenham Festival. Indeed, with just two placed efforts in 2015, *Gallant Oscar*'s third in the Grade 3 *Ultima Business Solutions Handicap Chase* and *God's Own* second to *Un De Sceaux* in the *Racing Post Arkle Challenge Trophy Chase*, **Oscar** breds have failed to provide us with a festival winner for two years running. Admittedly, **Oscar**'s representatives also failed to deliver us with a victory at the 2011 Cheltenham Festival, but at least six of the 15 who took part that year went close by securing place dividends, including *Peddlers Cross* and *Oscar Whisky* finishing 2nd and 3rd respectively in the *Stan James Champion Hurdle Challenge Trophy* and *Rock On Ruby* missing out in the *Neptune Investment Management Novices' Hurdle* by a short head.

Of the 14 **Oscar** bred participants at last year's festival, it could be said that three of them at least provided punters with a run for their money by finishing just outside the place positions. It was the *Charlie Longsdon* trained, *Our Kaempfer*, who came closest to winning some money for **Oscar** supporters, when he secured fifth spot and just a ½ length outside the places in the *Pertemps*

Network Final, a listed handicap hurdle run over a distance of three miles. In 6th position, at odds of 40/1 and a further ½ length behind *Our Kaempfer*, was another **Oscar** bred runner, the *Eoin Griffin* trained, **Rathpatrick**. The highest place that **Oscar**'s offspring achieved at the 2016 Cheltenham Festival was 4th, courtesy of *God's Own*, who at odds of 20/1 finished five lengths outside of the places in the *Betway Queen Mother Champion Chase*.

Going back to *Our Kaempfer*, he was the shortest price of all of **Oscar**'s offspring that took part at last year's festival, being the only **Oscar** bred festival runner with single figure odds when going off at 9/1. Indeed, some may claim that the circumstances at the 2016 Cheltenham Festival were similar to those in 2005, namely that the majority of **Oscar**'s progeny that took part last year, ran at big starting prices. And, it is true that 11 of the 14 **Oscar** sired runners went off at odds ranging from 20/1 to 50/1. However, I would counter this on the basis that in analysing the performance of **Oscar**'s offspring at Cheltenham Festivals over the past decade, and irrespective of the runners' starting prices, it is not unreasonable to have expected one or more of last year's 14 runners to have secured at least a place dividend. Looking at the table above, over the past ten Cheltenham Festivals, **Oscar**'s progeny have provided us with a win strike rate of 9% and a win and place strike rate of 23%, which means that we can expect a victory in close to one in every 10 runs and a win/place dividend in almost one in every four runs. But in 2016, **Oscar**'s offspring scored a duck. Put simply, **Oscar** sired horses under-performed at last year's Cheltenham Festival.

Within this Guide, there are a number of examples where the analysis of a sire's festival record, based upon the performance of that sire's offspring, will conclude that the starting prices of the runners appear to be a very significant factor in deciding whether or not a sire's progeny will run well. This is not the case with **Oscar**. In the last ten Cheltenham Festivals, **Oscar**'s progeny have recorded 29 win and place positions (11 wins and 18 places), eight of which were rewarded with odds of between 20/1 and 50/1. A further nine of the win and place positions were settled at odds of between 10/1 and 16/1. Just four of the victories and eight of the place positions were at single figure odds.

Despite the disappointment of 2016, **Oscar**'s progeny consistently deliver at Cheltenham Festivals, and it is due to the rewarding odds returned, that if one had blindly backed all 125 of **Oscar**'s offspring to have appeared at the festival from 2007 onwards, it would have resulted in a £5.38 profit to a £1.00 win stake. Interestingly, if one had decided to only back the progeny in the festival's non-handicap races and ignore **Oscar** bred runners in all of the handicap events, the aforementioned small profit is significantly enhanced to £33.38 to a £1.00 win stake. I cannot provide a logical explanation, but when it comes to the Cheltenham Festival, **Oscar**'s offspring have a far less impressive record in the handicap events. In total, **Oscar** sired runners have lined up in 44 festival handicap races and only *Oscar Park*, in the 2007 *Pertemps Final* has managed to cross the line in first. The record for place positions is also uninspiring with just 5 place dividends from those 44 runs. As a punter, therefore, it makes perfect sense to give the cold shoulder to **Oscar** breds that are entered in the festival's handicap races.

In studying **Oscar**'s statistics within specific race categories, we need to highlight the progeny's performance in two of the festival's prestigious hurdle races. **Oscar**'s offspring have performed remarkably well in the two mile *Champion Hurdle* with a very impressive record of a 1st, 2nd twice, 3rd, 6th and 12th from just six runs. The other hurdle race where **Oscar**'s offspring have a strong record is the *Neptune Investment Management Novices' Hurdle* over 2m5f. Of eight runs in the *Neptune*, seven of **Oscar**'s progeny have finished in the top seven positions, the finishing positions being 1,2,2,3,4,6,7 and 11 with SPs ranging from 4/1 to 18/1. With these impressive figures, it is a shame that we have to go back to 2013 for the last time that **Oscar**'s offspring had a runner in either of these two Grade 1 races, which was when *Rock On Ruby* finished runner-up to *Hurricane Fly* in the *Stan James Champion Hurdle Challenge Trophy*. If any **Oscar** sired horses are among the list of runners in either of these events at the 2017 Cheltenham Festival, then I advise punters to take them seriously.

Over fences, we will start with the two and a half mile chase category, where in twelve attempts to date, the closest that **Oscar**'s progeny have come to secure a top three position was in the 2014 *JLT Novices' Chase*, when **Felix Yonger** finished 4th as the 7/2 favourite. Avoid **Oscar**'s representatives over the bigger obstacles that are run within the 2½ mile category.

In the festival's two mile chases over the past 10 years, **Oscar**'s progeny have achieved a 50% win and place strike rate which is primarily down to **Big Zeb** who is responsible for four of the ten **Oscar** sired runners to have taken part in this category. *Big Zeb*, trained by *Colm Murphy*, ran in the *Queen Mother Champion Chase* between 2009 and 2012 and having won the event in 2010, followed up with two placed efforts in the next two renewals. The other two placed efforts in 2m chases were rewarded with big prices. In 2015, along with 10 others, *God's Own*, trained by *Tom George* and ridden by *Paddy Brennan*, took on the highly fancied *Un De Sceaux* in the *Racing Post Arkle Challenge Trophy Chase*. The *Willie Mullins* trained 4/6 favourite was never in any danger, but it was **God's Own**, at 33/1, who came closest, beaten by six lengths. The other placed effort came at an even bigger price, when **Askthemaster** (50/1) finished runner-up to *Oiseau De Nuit* in the 2011 running of the *Johnny Henderson Grand Annual Chase Challenge Cup*.

Now here is an interesting statistic. If one had placed a £1.00 each-way bet on every **Oscar** sired runner to line up in all three mile chases at the past five Cheltenham Festivals, it would have resulted in a £29.85 profit. The size of the profit is courtesy of three recent festival victories, with the progeny enjoying two consecutive *RSA Chase* victories with **Lord Windermere** at 8/1 in 2013 and **O'Faolains Boy** at 14/1 in 2014. This was followed by **Lord Windermere**'s Betfred Cheltenham Gold Cup Chase victory in 2014 at odds of 20/1. In addition to these three wins, one could make a strong case that **Oscar**'s offspring are rather unfortunate not to have recorded four 3m chase successes within the past five years, as it was in the 2013 renewal of the Foxhunters that **Oscar Delta** (20/1) was staying on and maintaining about a 4 lengths advantage, when the horse suddenly jinked left and unseated jockey, *Jane Mangan*, just 150 yards from the finishing line. So, the record in three mile festival chases in the past five years reads as 3 wins and 2 places from a total of 17 runs. It is interesting to note that before the 2012 Cheltenham Festival, the record of **Oscar**'s offspring in three mile chases was rather discouraging with just two placed efforts from 13 attempts, courtesy of **Offshore Account**'s 4th place in the 2010 *William Hill Trophy Handicap Chase* and **Oscar Delta** securing 3rd place in the 2011 *Christie's Foxhunter Chase Challenge Cup*.

To complete the picture for performances over fences, I would certainly not be put off in backing **Oscar**'s progeny in the *National Hunt Chase* which is for amateur riders and run over a distance of four miles. **Oscar** bred runners have won twice in their five runs to date, with victories secured by **Tricky Trickster** at 11/1 in 2009, and **Teaforthree**, the *Rebecca Curtis* trained 5/1 favourite, in 2012.

Despite the disappointing results for the offspring at the 2016 Cheltenham Festival, overall I am a supporter of **Oscar**'s progeny and come March 2017, based upon the past decade's results, I shall be especially interested in any **Oscar** sired runner that is listed amongst the runners in three of the first eight festival races. These races are the *Stan James Champion Hurdle Challenge Trophy* and the *Toby Balding National Hunt Chase* that take place on the opening day of the festival, followed by Wednesday's opening event, the *Neptune Investment Management Novices' Hurdle*. I would not be put off in supporting **Oscar**'s offspring in other festival races either, although I would advise punters to stay clear of all the handicap races and any chase event run in the 2½ category, where in a combined total of 50 festival races to date, **Oscar** supporters have been rewarded with just one victory and five places.

Poliglote (GB)

Quote from the 2016 Cheltenham Festival Stallion Guide - "Four victories and four place dividends from just 22 runs, represents an impressive Cheltenham Festival strike rate and supporters of **Poliglote**'s offspring can expect a return on their bets from one in every three races."

Poliglote (25-y-o)							
Race Format	Miles	Won	Placed	Unplaced	Total	Win %	Place %
	About 2m	0	3	4	7	0%	43%
Hurdles	About 2m 4f	2	1	4	7	29%	43%
	About 3m	0	0	2	2	0%	0%
	About 2m	0	0	2	2	0%	0%
Chases	About 2m 4f	0	0	3	3	0%	0%
	About 3m	1	1	2	4	25%	50%
	About 4m	1	0	1	2	50%	50%
Bumper	About 2m	0	0	0	0	-	-
Total		**4**	**5**	**18**	**27**	**15%**	**33%**

Despite failing to deliver a winner from five representatives at last year's meeting, **Poliglote**'s progeny still have an impressive Cheltenham Festival win strike rate of 15% which is the second highest strike rate of any stallion whose offspring have amassed at least 20 or more runs at the festival over the past decade.

Over the past decade, fourteen **Poliglote** sired runners have lined up in the festival's 2m and 2½m hurdle contests; events in which the offspring have performed particularly well. Nine of the runs resulted in a top 5 finish, including two victories, three runner-up spots and a 3rd place. *Spirit River* was the first of **Poliglote**'s stock to race in a Cheltenham Festival hurdle race, and perhaps provided a pointer as to the success or otherwise of the progeny, when he stayed on well to win the 2010 *Coral Cup* by 4½ lengths at odds of 14/1. It took four more years before a **Poliglote** bred runner would record the second hurdle festival victory, and once again, it was in a handicap event over 2½ miles. In only his fifth ever race, the *Willie Mullins* trained, *Don Poli*, was victorious at odds of 12/1, in the *Martin Pipe Conditional Jockeys' Handicap Hurdle*. The winner, ridden by conditional rider, *Mikey Fogarty*, secured the third victory of the day for *Gigginstown House Stud*, following the earlier successes of *Tiger Roll* (10/1) in the *JCB Triumph Hurdle* and *Very Wood* (33/1) in the *Albert Bartlett Novices' Hurdle*. When *Savello* (16/1) won the last race of the day, the *Johnny Henderson Grand Annual Chase Challenge Cup*, it capped off an extraordinary day for the owners who were celebrating an 82,653/1 four timer.

The following season after his festival hurdle victory, **Don Poli** arrived at the 2015 Cheltenham Festival to take his chance over the bigger obstacles in the 2015 *RSA Chase* over a distance of 3m½f. Towards the end of the race, four from home, the *Bryan Cooper* ridden 13/8 favourite, was clearly travelling the best of the contenders and so it proved, as he romped home to win by 6 lengths from *Southfield Theatre*. Last season, **Don Poli** lined up with eight others for the showpiece *Timico Cheltenham Gold Cup Chase*. He was held up and well off the pace for much of the race, and despite staying on from the third last to eventually secure 3rd place, he was never a threat to the front pair. For the record, the only other Cheltenham Festival chase victory for **Poliglote**'s progeny, occurred when the *Jonjo O'Neill* trained, **Butler's Cabin**, at 33/1, won the 2007 *National Hunt Chase Challenge Cup* over a distance of four miles.

Even though the five **Poliglote** bred horses that took part at last year's festival were unable to pick up a win, it certainly wasn't a disaster for the progeny, considering that four of the runners managed to secure a top six finishing spot. To date, supporters of **Poliglote**'s stock have been rewarded with a return on their bets for one in every three festival races, and with a 15% win strike rate to boot, that's good enough for me. A profit of £35.90 to a £1.00 each way stake, had one backed every single one of the 28 **Poliglote** sired festival runners, is not to be sniffed at. Come the 2017 Cheltenham Festival, it is a given that **Poliglote**'s progeny should be treated with the utmost respect.

Presenting (GB)

Quote from the 2016 Cheltenham Festival Stallion Guide - "In last year's Guide, I advised that it was worth making a note of any **Presenting** sired runner in the *Neptune Investment Management Novices' Hurdle*, as in nine attempts from the 2005 festival onwards, five of **Presenting**'s offspring had finished in the first 4 places, including one winner, *First Lieutenant* in 2011. In last season's renewal, *Snow Falcon* at 20/1 was the sole representative sired by **Presenting**, and he ran very well to finish in fifth position."

Race Format	Miles	Won	Placed	Unplaced	Total	Win %	Place %
				Presenting (25-y-o)			
	About 2m	0	3	5	8	0%	38%
Hurdles	About 2m 4f	2	1	20	23	9%	13%
	About 3m	2	2	14	18	11%	22%
	About 2m	0	0	9	9	0%	0%
	About 2m 4f	2	5	15	22	9%	32%
Chases	About 3m	6	10	31	47	13%	34%
	About 4m	0	1	19	20	0%	5%
Bumper	About 2m	1	1	13	15	7%	13%
Total		**13**	**23**	**126**	**162**	**8%**	**22%**

Before last season's *Neptune Investment Management Novices' Hurdle,* many tipsters had decided that the race would end up being a match between the front two in the market. As it turned out, the tipsters were spot on, but more difficult for punters, perhaps, was predicting whether it would be *Yanworth* or *Yorkhill* who would come out on top to win the race. On the face of it, a strong case could be made for the *JP McManus* owned *Yanworth* on the basis that 4 winners of the *Neptune* since 1998 had recorded a top six finish in the previous year's festival bumper and *Yanworth* had finished fourth in the 2015 running of the event. In addition, *Yanworth* had raced over hurdles exactly three times and so was firmly in line with 25 of the past 29 winners who had all previously run at least three times over hurdles. His rival, *Yorkhill*, on the other hand, had only experienced hurdles twice previously. And if you are one of many who consider previous Cheltenham form to be an advantage when it comes to picking festival winners, then that was another factor pointing towards *Yanworth* who had not only raced in the 2015 *Weatherbys Champion Bumper* but had also won the Grade 2 *Classic Novices Hurdle* at Cheltenham at the end of January. For *Yorkhill*, Cheltenham was virgin territory.

Alan King, Yanworth's trainer, is highly respected and has won several Cheltenham Festival races although the *Neptune* had so far eluded him. *Yorkhill*'s trainer, on the other hand, the hugely successful *Willie Mullins*, had won the *Neptune* on three previous occasions with *Fiveforthree* in 2008, *Mikael D'Haguenet* in 2009 and *Faugheen* in 2014. One other positive for *Yorkhill* supporters was the gelding's breeding, having been sired by **Presenting**. As highlighted in last year's Guide, **Presenting**'s offspring had an excellent record in the *Neptune*, recording 6 top five finishes from 10 attempts in the race. Any conclusions as to the success or otherwise of *Yanworth*'s sire at Cheltenham Festivals was a non-starter as the one and only run from *Norse Dancer*'s progeny was *Yanworth* himself when finishing 4th in the 2015 *Weatherbys Champion Bumper.*

Even though *Yanworth* started as the 11/10 favourite, it was *Yorkhill* at 3/1 and ridden by *Ruby Walsh*, who won the race relatively comfortably, beating *Yanworth* by 1¾ lengths, and in so doing, providing **Presenting**'s progeny with their second *Neptune* victory following *First Lieutenant*'s victory in 2011. Having been represented eleven times in this specific race, **Presenting**'s offspring have now managed to record a top five finish on seven occasions and so, quite clearly, we should look very seriously at any runner sired by **Presenting** in the 2017 running of this race.

There were 22 horses sired by **Presenting** that ran at last season's Cheltenham Festival and *Yorkhill* was the solitary winner, thereby continuing the recent trend of **Presenting**'s progeny of providing one victory per festival. *Yorkhill*'s success was preceded by *Rajdhani Express* (2013), *Present View* (2014) and *Call The Cops* (2015). With just 4 winners in the past five years, the success of **Presenting** as a Cheltenham Festival stallion is tailing off somewhat, with a win strike rate of just under 5%. The first five years of the past decade (2007-2011) shows far better success with 9 winners and a win strike rate of more than 11%. The view that **Presenting**'s progeny may not be the force of old is reinforced by analysing the past decade's 23 place positions, where the data tells a similar story to the win strike rate. Between 2007 and 2011, 16 place positions represents a 20% place strike rate and a 31% win and place strike rate, compared with 7 place positions in the past five festivals resulting in a 8½% place strike rate and a 13% win and place strike rate.

In looking at the past decade of festivals, 100 of **Presenting**'s progeny have registered 162 runs between them which is more than any other Stallion (**Oscar** comes next with 125 runs). Without doubt, *Denman* is the most renowned of **Presenting**'s offspring. Having finished runner-up to *Nicanor* in the 2006 *Royal & SunAlliance Novices' Hurdle*, he then registered two chase wins, first in the 2007 *Royal & SunAlliance Chase* and then in the *totesport Cheltenham Gold Cup Chase* the following year. He then went on to finish runner-up in the *Gold Cup* for the next three years (2009 through to 2011). In addition to *Denman*, other notable Cheltenham winners sired by **Presenting** are *Weapon's Amnesty* (twice), *Ballabriggs, Dunguib, First Lieutenant* and *War of Attrition*.

Of the past decade's 162 festival runs from **Presenting** sired horses, six of the 13 wins have been achieved in a three mile chase, which calculates into a 13% win strike rate from the 47 attempts within this race category. If we add the 10 place positions that have also been earned, it results into a 34% win and place strike rate or a one in three chance of receiving a return every time one places a bet on the offspring in a three mile chase. However, we need to be very mindful of what has been achieved within the past five years, as it has a significant impact on the aforementioned strike rates. For starters, in 25 attempts in three mile chases over the past five years, **Presenting**'s runners have failed to record a victory. All six wins in the above table were recorded between 2007 and 2011. Indeed, these last five blank years have had an impact on the profitability of backing **Presenting**'s offspring in three mile chases at the festival. In the 2015 Cheltenham Festival Stallion Guide, I advised that a £1.00 win bet on all of **Presenting**'s offspring to line up in three mile chases at the festival in the past decade would have returned a £51.95 profit. In last year's Guide, that £51.95 figure had been reduced to a £46.95 profit. If we calculate the outcome today, then a £1 win bet on every **Presenting** sired runner to have run in 3m chases in the past ten years would result in a £34.45 profit. Or put another way, one can say that a £1 win bet on every **Presenting** sired runner to have run in 3m chases in the past five years would have resulted in a £25.00 loss!

Based on the above information, should we now abandon all thoughts of supporting **Presenting**'s representatives in three mile chases? In my view, the answer is no. Or more specifically, I believe punters should still be interested in the offspring provided they are towards the front of the betting market. Over the past five years, of the 25 **Presenting** sired horses to have appeared in the 3m chase category, nine of them lined up at starting prices between 5/2 and 16/1. Of those, three finished 2nd at prices of 16/1, 14/1 and 9/2 and three ran into 4th of which just one resulted in a paid placed dividend. Not one of the progeny's sixteen runners with a starting price of 20/1 or greater have finished in the first four. The closest that **Presenting**'s offspring came to adding to *Yorkhill*'s victory last year was in the *Fulke Walwyn Kim Muir Challenge Cup Handicap Chase*, when **A Good Skin** at 14/1, trained by *Tom George*, took the runner-up spot behind *Cause of Causes* who was out the back and struggling for much of the race before jockey *Jamie Codd* managed to galvanise his horse to burst onto the scene late on, before running on strongly to win by 12 lengths.

In last year's Guide, I advised punters to be wary of backing **Presenting**'s representatives in the shortest and longest chase events at the festival. The combined result of all two and four mile chase events in the past decade has resulted in the offspring recording just one place from 29 attempts. Last year, **Southfield Royale** lined up as the 5/1 favourite in the 4m *146th Year Of The National Hunt Chase Challenge Cup* but finished 4th and five lengths outside of the places, having blundered two fences out. The other **Presenting** sired runner in the race, *Pleasant Company* (25/1), was pulled up. Two of **Presenting**'s offspring took part in the final race of the festival, the *Johnny Henderson Grand Annual Chase Challenge Cup*, run over a distance of 2m62y. The finishing positions of 13th (**Dunraven Storm** at 50/1) and 18th (**Bright New Dawn** at 16/1) means that all 10 (9 in the past decade) of **Presenting**'s efforts in the festival's two mile chase events have resulted in nothing better than the 5th place achieved by **Another Promise** in the 2007 *Irish Independent Arkle Challenge Trophy Chase*.

Over hurdles, **Presenting**'s stock have an unimpressive record with four wins in 49 attempts, and if you take out the *Neptune* as covered at the top of this commentary, then the result is just two wins from 41 festival hurdle runs. Further analysis, however, shows that in those 41 hurdle races within the past decade, only eleven runners were sent off at single figure odds, so if one had supported every **Presenting** sired runner over hurdles with an SP of under 10/1, the two winners would have given a profit of £8.00 to a £1.00 win stake. In addition to these two victories (**Weapon's Amnesty** at 8/1 in the 2009 *Albert Bartlett Novices' Hurdle* and **Call The Cops** at 9/1 in the 2015 *Pertemps Network Final*), a further four runners managed to secure a place dividend. So, for those who have a preference for betting each way, the profit would have been slightly lower at £5.05 to a £1.00 each way stake.

In conclusion, it is clear that over the past five Cheltenham Festivals, **Presenting**'s representatives are not meeting the same level of success that the offspring achieved between 2007 and 2011. Even so, provided punters are selective, there is still a case to support the progeny. In the festival's 3m chase category, I sense that a victory is long overdue, and **Presenting**'s offspring have been knocking at the door recently with a couple of runner-up spots. So, I am interested in the progeny's runners in these events provided the odds are under 20/1. I will also take note of **Presenting** sired runners at the front of the market (single figure odds) in the festival's hurdle races. And finally, with seven top five finishes, including two wins, from 11 runs in the event, I will look out for any **Presenting** sired runner who lines up in the 2017 *Neptune Investment Management Novices Hurdle*.

Robin Des Champs (FR)

Quote from the 2016 Cheltenham Festival Stallion Guide - "**Robin Des Champs** is just 19 years old, and on the basis that he remains alive and well, I'm convinced that in the years to come, we will witness many more Cheltenham Festival victories from the progeny of this record breaking sire."

Robin Des Champs (20-y-o)

Race Format	Miles	Won	Placed	Unplaced	Total	Win %	Place %
	About 2m	1	0	6	7	14%	14%
Hurdles	About 2m 4f	7	0	4	11	64%	64%
	About 3m	0	1	4	5	0%	20%
	About 2m	0	0	1	1	0%	0%
Chases	About 2m 4f	3	0	1	4	75%	75%
	About 3m	1	1	3	5	20%	40%
	About 4m	0	0	0	0	-	-
Bumper	About 2m	0	0	5	5	0%	0%
Total		**12**	**2**	**24**	**38**	**32%**	**37%**

It was another successful meeting for **Robin Des Champs'** progeny at the 2016 Cheltenham Festival. With last year's two wins, the offspring have had at least one winner at every festival going back to 2009. The most renowned of **Robin Des Champs'** stock is the mare, *Quevega*. Trained by *Willie Mullins*, *Quevega* won 16 of her 24 races, earning almost £750,000 in prize money. At Cheltenham, she won the *David Nicholson Mares' Hurdle* a record six times in a row, beating the previous record set by *Golden Miller's* five consecutive *Gold Cups* in the 1930s. With six victories, *Quevega* is responsible for half of the progeny's Cheltenham Festival wins, double the number of wins of another distinguished **Robin Des Champs** bred horse, the ill-fated *Vautour*.

In the 2016 Stallion Guide, I highlighted how impressed I had been with *Vautour's* two festival runs to date, these being a six lengths success over *Josses Hill* in the 2014 *Sky Bet Supreme Novices' Hurdle* and an awe-inspiring victory, by 15 lengths, in the 2015 JLT *Novices' Chase*. By running away with the *Ryanair Chase* at last year's meeting, and perhaps justifying the decision to bypass the *Timico Cheltenham Gold Cup Chase*, *Vautour* made it three festival successes in a row. In my view, there was a good chance that *Vautour* would make it four wins at the 2017 Festival, but with the devastating news of his death on 6th November 2016, it is not to be. In what must have been a freak accident whilst out in a paddock, *Vautour* was found to have a broken foreleg and the vet had no option but to put him down. The five-time Grade 1 winner was victorious in ten of his 16 career starts and finished out of the first two only once, when falling at *Aintree* in last year's Grade 1 *JLT Melling Chase*.

Quevega and *Vautour*, quite clearly, have had a very significant and positive impact on the rather enormous 32% win strike rate of **Robin Des Champs'** offspring. Nevertheless, even if we take these two champions out of calculations, the win strike rate is still very good at just over 10%. Only two other stallions whose progeny have amassed thirty festival runs or more within the past ten years, have attained a win-rate of more than 10%, these being *Westerner* (13%) and *King's Theatre* (12%).

Ten of the 12 **Robin Des Champs** sired winners were sent off as the market leader for their respective festival races, nine as the outright favourite, and *Vautour*, the 7/2 joint favourite in the

2014 *Sky Bet Supreme Novices' Hurdle*. The biggest price favourite, at odds of 9/2, was *Sir Des Champs* in the 2011 *Martin Pipe Conditional Jockeys' Handicap Hurdle* and he won again the following season, this time as the 3/1 second favourite, when taking victory in the 2012 *Jewson Novices Chase*. With eleven festival successes at odds of less than 9/2, it was a welcome change at last year's meeting to see a **Robin Des Champs** bred horse enter the Winners Enclosure at a starting price in double figures. The winner was *Un Temps Pour Tout*, who took the honours in the Grade 3 *Ultima Handicap Chase* at odds of 11/1. In securing victory, not only did *Un Temps Pour Tout* become the biggest priced winner for the progeny at a Cheltenham Festival, he also became the first **Robin Des Champs** sired winner to be trained by someone other than *Willie Mullins*, from whose stable hailed the other three victors - *Quevega*, *Vautour* and *Sir Des Champs*. Having trained *Un Temps Pour Tout* to victory in the *Ultima Handicap Chase*, which was the third race of the entire festival meeting, *David Pipe* must have been hopeful of another winner in the 25 contests to follow. However, it wasn't to be and he had to be content with the *Tom Scudamore* ridden, *Un Temps Pour Tout*, being his sole 2016 Cheltenham Festival winner.

Without doubt, last year was by far the most successful Cheltenham Festival meeting for **Robin Des Champs** bred outsiders, where not only did we see an 11/1 winner but also four more horses at odds of 12/1 or greater, recording a top six finish. Before last year's meeting, ten of the 13 of the offspring, that lined up at odds of 10/1 or greater, were unable to finish higher than eighth. The sole top six placing came from *Tour Des Champs*, who just missed out by a neck in securing a place dividend, when finishing 5th in the 2014 *Baylis & Harding Affordable Luxury Handicap Chase* at odds of 11/1. In other words, for **Robin Des Champs** sired festival runners that had an SP of 10/1 or greater, the strike rate for a top six placing between 2008 and 2015, was just 8%. Contrast this with the top 6 hit rate of 62% at the 2016 Festival, where eight of the nine entries sired by **Robin Des Champs**, lined up at double figure odds with five of them finishing in the first five. And the SPs were big. The previously highlighted *Un Temps Pour Tout* won at 11/1; *Champers On Ice* took 3rd spot at 20/1 in the *Albert Bartlett Novices' Hurdle*; 25/1 shot, *Robins Reef* finished 4th in the *Trull House Stud Mares' Novices' Hurdle*; *Tombstone* (12/1) also passed the post in 4th in the *Sky Bet Supreme Novices' Hurdle*; and at 28/1, *Welsh Shadow* secured 5th place in the *Neptune Investment Management Novices' Hurdle*. Incidentally, the three runners who didn't make the first five had SPs of 40/1, 66/1 and 100/1. Only time will tell whether the 2016 festival was a one-off, or whether it is a marker of better things to come for **Robin Des Champs** bred outsiders. My money is on the latter.

At just 20 years old, with 12 festival winners already in the bag, and an incredibly impressive 32% win strike rate, I am loathe to discount any **Robin Des Champs** bred runner at the 2017 Cheltenham Festival. Supporters can be forgiven for deciding a "no bet" on the offspring's entries where the odds are perhaps 40/1 or more, and also potentially in Wednesday's *Weatherbys Champion Bumper*, where from the five attempts in the race so far, 13th is the highest position achieved. Outside of these circumstances, to date, for every five **Robin Des Champs** sired horses that have faced the starter in a festival event, two of them crossed the winning line in first place. That is some statistic. Betting on **Robin Des Champs**' progeny at Cheltenham Festivals is a no-brainer.

Saddler Maker (IRE)

Saddler Maker was not featured in the 2016 Cheltenham Festival Stallion Guide.

Saddler Maker (Died as an 18-y-o in 2016)

Race Format	Miles	Won	Placed	Unplaced	Total	Win %	Place %
	About 2m	0	2	1	3	0%	67%
Hurdles	About 2m 4f	0	0	1	1	0%	0%
	About 3m	0	1	0	1	0%	100%
	About 2m	0	0	0	0	-	-
	About 2m 4f	0	2	0	2	0%	100%
Chases	About 3m	0	0	0	0	-	-
	About 4m	0	0	0	0	-	-
Bumper	About 2m	0	0	0	0	-	-
Total		**0**	**5**	**2**	**7**	**0%**	**71%**

It is definitely questionable as to why I have included **Saddler Maker** in the 2017 Cheltenham Festival Stallion Guide. With the progeny having had just seven festival runs so far, one needs to be extremely cautious about making any hasty judgements about the success or otherwise on future festival runs from the offspring. That said, considering the fact that the seven festival appearances have been made by six of **Saddler Maker**'s brood (rather than 1 or 2 of the stock dominating the statistics), the 71% win and place strike rate is phenomenal. It should also be pointed out that six of those seven festival runs took place at the 2016 Cheltenham Festival, and so one can anticipate a reasonable number of **Saddler Maker** sired entries for this year too.

In short, **Saddler Maker**'s offspring is suffering from "seconditis". **Bouvreuil** kicked it all off, when being the only one of the progeny to be represented at the 2015 Cheltenham Festival, he finished runner-up in the *Fred Winter Juvenile Handicap Hurdle*, at a starting price of 14/1. It was a very satisfactory race for *Paul Nicholls*, who trained both **Bouvreuil** and the winner, *Qualando*, rewarding exacta backers of these two horses, with a dividend of £481.40.

In entering the five year old, **Bouvreuil**, in the 2016 listed *Close Brothers Novices' Handicap Chase*, *Paul Nicholls* was attempting to emulate his one and only success in this event, when seven years previously, his stable's *Chapoturgeon* became the only five year old to win the race. When **Bouvreuil** took a narrow advantage at the last, it looked as though the 14/1 shot may be the second five year old to win the race, but his 9 year old rival, *Ballyalton*, rallied and regained the lead in the final 120 yards to leave **Bouvreuil** to finish with a runner-up spot for the second year in a row.

Two days later and **Saddler Maker**'s two representatives on the Thursday also found one too good in their respective races. In the opening *JLT Novices' Chase*, **Bristol De Mai** was one of three 4/1 co-favourites, when finishing 2nd and some 3 lengths adrift of the winner, *Black Hercules*. Just over two hours later, the *Colin Tizzard* trained, *Thistlecrack*, was making a mockery of the opposition in the *Ryanair World Hurdle*, when winning impressively. The 8/1 runner-up in the 3m event, and some 7 lengths behind the winner was the **Saddler Maker** sired, **Alpha Des Obeaux**, trained by *Mouse Morris*, who less than a month later was all over our television screens and newspapers, having trained *Aintree*'s *Crabbie's Grand National Chase* winner, *Rule The World*.

The run of 2nd place finishes for **Saddler Maker**'s progeny continued at last year's festival meeting in Friday's opening event, the *JCB Triumph Hurdle*, when ***Apple's Jade*** became yet another of the offspring, who was unable to quicken when it mattered. Despite leading after the last, the *Willie Mullins* trained 12/1 chance, was no match for the fast finishing favourite, *Ivanovich Gorbatov*, who quickened away in the final 110 yards, to win by 1¼ lengths.

It is a fantastic start for the stock of **Saddler Maker** to have already achieved five runner-up positions from just seven festival runs and if you happen to strongly fancy a **Saddler Maker** bred runner come the spring, then I would not dissuade you from placing a bet. However, when it comes to future Cheltenham Festivals, I think it wise to ask ourselves the following questions. Can we expect the same ratio of success from the progeny? Can **Saddler Maker**'s offspring improve on those 2nd places and start to provide festival winners? Does the progeny lack an extra gear when it comes to the business end of the race, up the Cheltenham Hill? Unfortunately, these questions will remain unanswered until more substantive evidence is provided, which will only become available by analysing the performances of **Saddler Maker** bred runners at forthcoming festivals. Therefore, at the 2017 Cheltenham Festival, my advice is to resist placing a bet and observe the offspring instead.

Saint Des Saints (FR)

Quote from the 2016 Cheltenham Festival Stallion Guide - "I am a huge fan of **Saint Des Saints'** offspring and although there are only sixteen runs on the board, the evidence to date strongly suggests that the progeny perform extremely well at Cheltenham Festivals."

Saint Des Saints (19-y-o)							
Race Format	*Miles*	*Won*	*Placed*	*Unplaced*	*Total*	*Win %*	*Place %*
Hurdles	About 2m	0	4	1	5	0%	80%
	About 2m 4f	1	0	3	4	25%	25%
	About 3m	0	0	2	2	0%	0%
Chases	About 2m	0	0	1	1	0%	0%
	About 2m 4f	1	0	2	3	33%	33%
	About 3m	0	3	4	7	0%	43%
	About 4m	0	0	0	0	-	-
Bumper	About 2m	0	1	1	2	0%	50%
Total		**2**	**8**	**14**	**24**	**8%**	**42%**

At last year's meeting, it was always going to be difficult for the progeny of **Saint Des Saints** to equal, let alone exceed, the performance heights that were achieved at the 2015 Cheltenham Festival, in which all five **Saint Des Saints** bred participants finished in the first four of their respective races. Nevertheless, I was still a little disappointed that the offspring was unable to add a winner from the eight runners that were entered in last year's festival races. In addition, preceding last year, **Saints Des Saints'** stock had the enviable record of all thirteen of its runners who had managed to get round in their races, attaining a top eight finish. Many analysts would conclude that had the three fallers stayed on their feet, they would have also hit a front eight position.

As it turned out, then, one would have to say that 2016 was a disappointing festival for **Saint Des Saints'** fans, despite the offspring attaining three place dividends from its eight runners. As for the progeny's attachment to a top eight finish, this statistic well and truly went out the window, with **Connetable's** 11th in the 2016 *JCB Triumph Hurdle*, **Days of Heaven** finishing 23rd in the *Coral Cup* and **The Saint James** being pulled up in the *Johnny Henderson Grand Annual Chase Challenge Cup*.

In last year's Stallion Guide, I mentioned that with a win and place strike rate of 44%, supporters of **Saint Des Saints'** offspring can expect a return on bets for close to one in every two races, and with three places from 8 runs last year, the 2016 win and place strike rate of 37.5% was reasonably near to the going rate. The first of those place positions arose on the second day of last year's festival in the *Fred Winter Juvenile Handicap Hurdle*, and it was so very close to being a win for the progeny. Having been in 4th place after the last, the *Paul Nicholls* trained **Romain De Senam** (20/1), ran on really strongly in the last 100 yards, just failing to catch the winner, *Diego Du Charmil*. The margin of victory was a head, but one or two more yards and **Romain De Senam** would have won.

On *Gold Cup* day, four **Saint Des Saints** sired horses were to race, the second of them being **Wait For Me** in the *Vincent O'Brien County Handicap Hurdle*. Trained by *Philip Hobbs*, the 7/1 joint favourite was always going to be beaten by the front two, but he ran well to finish 4th and a head behind his stablemate, *Sternrubin*. Two races later and it was the showpiece of the festival, the *Timico Cheltenham Gold Cup Chase*, where the **Saint Des Saints** bred, **Djakadam**, lined up as the joint 3rd favourite. It was *Djakadam*'s third race at a Cheltenham Festival. His first visit to Cheltenham was rather unlucky as he was running well and just behind the leader, when he fell four out in the 2014 running of the Grade 1 *JLT Novices' Chase*. His second race, in the 2015 *Gold Cup*, was a big improvement as he ran well to finish behind the novice, *Coneygree*.

It was perhaps inevitable that *Djakadam* wouldn't be able to go one better in the 2016 *Gold Cup* as it would have required him to overcome the very strong oddity that horses failing to win in their first *Gold Cup* attempt, were very unlikely to win the race if they tried again. Last year, four runners were unable to defy this statistic - *Djakadam*, *Carlingford Lough*, *Smad Place* and *On His Own*. In fact, the last horse to have won a *Gold Cup*, having been beaten on their first attempt, was *See More Business* in 1999. This century, 62 runners that were beaten on their *Gold Cup* debut have tried again and all of them have been beaten. *Djakadam* ran a very good race in the 2016 *Timico Cheltenham Gold Cup Chase*, but towards the end of the race, it was clear he wasn't going to trouble the victorious *Don Cossack*, and he was well beaten to take the runner-up spot for the second year in succession.

If we look at the festival performances of all 24 **Saint Des Saints** sired runners, then the obvious conclusion is that, for the most part, the progeny acquit themselves well at Cheltenham Festivals, as indicated by 62.5% of the runners attaining a top six position and a 42% win and place strike rate. In addition, those performances have been consistent across all race categories in which the offspring have raced. With 24 runs spread across the board, except for 4m chases, it is too early to determine whether a particular race category is more favourable than others, although I will highlight the results to date of the **Saint Des Saints'** sired four year olds.

I have already highlighted the 2016 *Fred Winter Juvenile Handicap Hurdle*, in which the 4 year old, **Romain De Senam**, finished runner-up. In the same race the previous season, *Paul Carberry* rode another **Saint Des Saints** bred 4 year old into a place, with *The Saint James* taking 3rd place behind the *Paul Nicholls* trained duo of *Qualando* and *Bouvreuil* who finished 1st and 2nd respectively. Two more of the progeny's 4 year olds have taken part in the *JCB Triumph Hurdle*. Last season, **Connetable** finished 11th at 14/1, but three years earlier, in the 2013 running, the *Paul Nicholls* trained, **Sametegal** secured third position behind stablemate *Far West* who finished 2nd behind the runaway winner, *Our Conor*. Not only have three out of four **Saint Des Saints** sired 4 year olds attained a place dividend at festival meetings, they have all done so at big prices. The starting price for **Romain de Senam** was 20/1, whilst the 3rd places of **Sametegal** and *The Saint James* were both gained at odds of 33/1.

In looking at the list of entries for the 2017 Cheltenham Festival, if you come across a runner sired by **Saint Des Saints**, bear in mind the following statistics from the progeny's 24 festival runs to date:

Ten of the 24 runs has resulted in a win or place dividend.
75% of four year old runners have secured a place dividend.
80% of the runners have secured a place in two mile hurdle events.
7 of 11 hurdle runs resulted in a top six finish.
6 of 11 chase runs resulted in a top six finish.
A 3rd and 4th placing in the two runs so far in the *Weatherbys Champion Bumper*.

Enough said?

Shantou (USA)

Quote from the 2016 Cheltenham Festival Stallion Guide - "The suggestion to punters is to take into account any of **Shantou**'s offspring that are entered in the 2016 Cheltenham Festival, especially in chases and in particular three mile chases."

Shantou (24-y-o)							
Race Format	*Miles*	*Won*	*Placed*	*Unplaced*	*Total*	*Win %*	*Place %*
	About 2m	0	0	3	3	0%	0%
Hurdles	About 2m 4f	0	2	2	4	0%	50%
	About 3m	0	1	6	7	0%	14%
	About 2m	0	0	0	0	-	-
Chases	About 2m 4f	1	0	2	3	33%	33%
	About 3m	0	4	1	5	0%	80%
	About 4m	0	1	1	2	0%	50%
Bumper	About 2m	1	0	0	1	100%	100%
Total		**2**	**8**	**15**	**25**	**8%**	**40%**

If you had placed a £1.00 each way bet on all eight of **Shantou**'s offspring that raced at the 2016 Cheltenham Festival, you would now be £3.80 better off. The previous season, in 2015, there were five **Shantou** sired participants, and adopting the same strategy of a £1.00 each way bet on all five festival runners would have been rewarded with a £2.20 profit. Adopting the same policy in 2013 and 2014 would have provided returns of £28.38 and £7.80 respectively. With a profitable track record at the past four festivals, it is crystal clear that **Shantou**'s progeny perform well when it comes to Cheltenham Festivals.

If we delve deeper into analysing the festival performances of the offspring, it is apparent that the progeny have the better record over fences. So far, we only have 10 chase contests on which to make some judgements, but the current position of 1 win and 5 placings is exceptional. *Ballynagour*, from *David Pipe*'s stable, is responsible for the offspring's three runs in the 2½ chase category. In 2013, he was a well-supported favourite in the *Byrne Group Plate* over 2m5f, but did not live up to expectations and finished 8th. However, in the following year's renewal of the race, at the more appealing price of 12/1, he made amends when he quickened clear, under jockey *Tom Scudamore*, to win by 8 lengths from *Colour Squadron*, the 5/1 favourite for the race. Having missed the 2015 festival, *David Pipe* entered **Ballynagour** in the same race for the third time in 2016. Now named the *Brown Advisory and Merribelle Stable Plate*, **Ballynagour**, 20/1 and now a 10 year old, ran a reasonable race to finish 7th, having been hampered at the 8th fence.

In five attempts in the festival's three mile chase category, **Shantou**'s progeny have managed to secure a place dividend four times. The first of those placings occurred in 2013 when **Super Duty**, the 11/2 favourite, finished runner-up when beaten by a head in the dying strides by *Same Difference* in the *Fulke Walwyn Kim Muir Challenge Cup Handicap Chase*. In the Grade 1 *RSA Chase*, **Shantou** sired horses have secured 3rd place twice. In 2014, **Morning Assembly**, ridden by *Davy Russell*, was six lengths adrift of the leading duo but still stayed on under pressure to take the last remaining place at odds of 9/1. And in 2015, it was turn of the *Noel Meade* trained, **Wounded Warrior** (12/1), to take 3rd spot when the horse, ridden by *Paul Carberry*, just managed to out battle the eventual 4th, *Adriana Des Mottes*, by a head. At the 2016 Cheltenham Festival, **Morning Assembly** secured a place in a three mile festival chase for a second time. On this occasion, trainer *Pat Fahy* entered the bay gelding in Tuesday's Grade 3 *Ultima Handicap Chase*, and the **Shantou** bred 9 year old did not disappoint supporters when managing to take a 4th place paid dividend at odds of 10/1.

At the 2016 meeting, **Shantou**'s progeny registered their first festival runners over a distance of four miles, when two **Shantou** sired horses lined up in the *146th Year of the National Hunt Chase Challenge Cup*. ***Shantou Flyer*** was in midfield when falling at the 18th flight, but ***Measureofmydreams***, ridden by *Katie Walsh*, the sister of *Ruby Walsh*, captured third place at odds of 9/1.

The results that have been achieved by **Shantou** sired runners over hurdles at the festival have been much more hit and miss. The progeny have yet to win a hurdle contest in fourteen runs over the smaller obstacles, but have managed to achieve three place positions at the rather rewarding SPs of 9/1, 20/1 and 50/1. The 50/1 outsider, trained by County Kildare based, *Alan Fleming*, was ***Tully East***, who finished 4th in the last season's renewal of the *Martin Pipe Conditional Jockeys' Handicap Hurdle*. The other two place positions for **Shantou**'s stock were both attained at the 2015 Cheltenham Festival. ***Polly Peachum,*** was just denied victory by a head in the *OLBG Mares' Hurdle*, and ***The Tourard Man*** stayed on well after the final hurdle, to take third place in the 2015 *Pertemps Network Final*.

Although there have only been two festival wins for **Shantou**'s stock, these being ***Briar Hill***'s 25/1 success in the 2013 *Weatherbys Champion Bumper* and ***Ballynagour***'s 12/1 victory in the 2014 *Byrne Group Plate*, as a result of the eight place dividends, the bottom line is that supporting **Shantou**'s progeny has been consistently profitable.

In conclusion, there are so many positives with regard to the performances of **Shantou** bred horses that have run at the Cheltenham Festival, not least the win and place strike rates, which read as 40% across all race categories, 60% in festival chase events and 80% if we take the 3m chase category alone. Moreover, from a financial perspective, backing all 25 **Shantou** sired festival runners at £1.00 each way would have produced a profit of £36.18. The data is beyond question. Punters will make a profit betting on **Shantou**'s offspring at Cheltenham Festivals.

Shirocco (GER)

Shirocco was not featured in the 2016 Cheltenham Festival Stallion Guide.

Race Format	*Miles*	*Won*	*Placed*	*Unplaced*	*Total*	*Win %*	*Place %*
	About 2m	2	0	1	3	67%	67%
Hurdles	About 2m 4f	0	0	5	5	0%	0%
	About 3m	0	1	0	1	0%	100%
	About 2m	0	0	0	0	-	-
Chases	About 2m 4f	0	0	0	0	-	-
	About 3m	0	0	0	0	-	-
	About 4m	1	0	0	1	100%	100%
Bumper	About 2m	0	0	0	0	-	-
Total		**3**	**1**	**6**	**10**	**30%**	**40%**

Shirocco (16-y-o)

Annie Power is the most well-known of **Shirocco**'s festival representatives, and it is perhaps a little disappointing that having been the favourite for all three starts, the mare has registered just one Cheltenham Festival victory. Indeed, at the time of writing, *Annie Power* has won 15 of her 17 races under Rules, her only defeats being at the 2014 and 2015 festival meetings. *Annie Power* made her festival debut in the 2014 *Ladbrokes World Hurdle* and when jockey *Ruby Walsh* was level with the *Barry Geraghty* ridden, *More Of That*, just before the last hurdle, many would have expected the 11/8 favourite to quicken away and win. But, it wasn't to be, and *More Of That* stayed on the better and was in command in the last 75 yards to win by 1½ lengths.

All the talk before the opening day of the 2015 festival surrounded the four favourites in Tuesday's four Grade 1 races, these being the *Sky Bet Supreme Novices Hurdle*; the *Racing Post Arkle Challenge Trophy Chase*; the *Stan James Champion Hurdle Challenge Trophy* and the *OLBG Mares' Hurdle*. All four favourites, trained by *Willie Mullins*, were to be ridden by the Cheltenham Festival's most successful jockey, *Ruby Walsh*, and so unsurprisingly, a huge number of bets had been placed on the four Irish-based runners, with some newspapers reporting accumulator bets from some 250,000 punters. Following *Douvan*'s success in the *Supreme* at 2/1, followed by *Un De Sceaux*'s 4/6 *Arkle* victory and then *Faugheen*'s impressive *Champion Hurdle* win at odds of 4/5, Britain's bookmakers were facing an estimated pay-out of millions of pounds. So when odds-on favourite, *Annie Power*, fell at the final hurdle of the *OLBG Mares' Hurdle*, thousands of punters were crying in their pints of Guinness and bookies averted what William Hill called "Armageddon Tuesday".

Last year, one month before the *Stan James Champion Hurdle Challenge Trophy* was due to be run, *Annie Power* was not being considered for the race. However, when news came in that stablemate, *Faugheen*, had suffered an injury and was out for the season, *Annie Power* suddenly became the *Champion Hurdle*'s new favourite. As expected, a week before the race, *Annie Power* was supplemented for the festival's showpiece hurdle event and for owner, *Susannah Ricci*, it was third time lucky as the 5/2 favourite made all and drew clear at the last to win impressively from *My Tent Or Yours*.

Like *Annie Power*, the *Paul Nicholls* trained, *Lac Fontana* has also raced at the Cheltenham Festival in three successive years, finishing mid-field in races either side of an 11/1 victory in the 2014 *Vincent O'Brien County Handicap Hurdle*. *Lac Fontana* was the first of **Shirocco**'s brood to make an appearance at a Cheltenham Festival when in 2013, at an SP of 25/1, he finished 8th in the *JCB Triumph Hurdle*. A year after his triumph in the *County Hurdle*, he went up in distance to 2m5f when running disappointingly to finish 9th in another highly competitive event, the *Coral Cup*. After missing all of the last campaign following a setback in October 2015, it is possible that *Lac Fontana* will appear in a Novice Chase at the 2017 Cheltenham Festival. He recently returned to action when finishing 8th in a handicap hurdle at *Newbury* on 31st December 2016.

With three runs apiece, *Annie Power* and *Lac Fontana* make up 60% of the festival outings from **Shirocco**'s offspring. The remaining four appearances of the progeny have come from *Red Sherlock*, *Mijhaar*, *Rock The Kasbah* and *Minella Rocco*. Having arrived at the 2014 Cheltenham Festival unbeaten from six starts, the *David Pipe* trained *Red Sherlock*, lined up in the *Neptune Investment Management Novices' Hurdle* as the 7/2 second favourite. As it turned out, he weakened coming up the hill and eventually finished ninth, being no match for the winning favourite, *Faugheen*. *Red Sherlock* hasn't raced since although there are some encouraging reports coming from the *David Pipe* yard that the *Johnson family* owned seven year old may be back in action in late January/early February 2017.

With two of **Shirocco**'s progeny performing poorly in the 2015 *Coral Cup* (*Lac Fontana* finishing 9th and *Mijhaar* a further four places back in 13th), **Shirocco** supporters were hopeful of a much more accomplished run from the *Philip Hobbs* trained, *Rock The Kasbah*, in the 2016 renewal. Despite being well fancied in the market, *Rock The Kasbah*, ran abysmally and of the 26 runners who set off, the 15/2 favourite came home in 22nd position.

At last year's Cheltenham Festival, all three **Shirocco** sired runners who participated, were well fancied in the market, although unlike *Anne Power* and *Rock The Kasbah*, the *Jonjo O'Neill* trained, *Minella Rocco*, was not the favourite of a hurdle event, but an 8/1 chance in a four mile chase event. The six year old provided **Shirocco**'s progeny with a second 2016 festival victory, when staying on well to see off the challenge of *Native River*, in the *146th Year Of The National Hunt Chase Challenge Cup*.

The table above makes good reading, and if it hadn't been for *Annie Power*'s fall at the last flight, when 4 lengths clear, in the 2015 *OLBG Mares' Hurdle*, then the already impressive win and place strike rates for **Shirocco**'s progeny would be even better. Nevertheless, a 30% win strike rate is a hugely encouraging statistic for this young stallion, as is the £14.50 profit to a £1.00 win stake had one backed all ten of the offspring's festival runs to date. It is still early days to make any ultra-confident predictions about **Shirocco** sired festival runners, but my expectation is that punters will continue to be rewarded by backing them.

Sinndar (IRE)

Quote from the 2016 Cheltenham Festival Stallion Guide - "Although yet to win a Cheltenham Festival race, **Sinndar**'s progeny have been consistently knocking at the door in the festival's two mile hurdle races."

Race Format	Miles	Won	Placed	Unplaced	Total	Win %	Place %
	Sinndar (20-y-o)						
Hurdles	About 2m	0	4	7	11	0%	36%
	About 2m 4f	0	0	1	1	0%	0%
	About 3m	0	1	1	2	0%	50%
Chases	About 2m	0	0	0	0	-	-
	About 2m 4f	0	0	0	0	-	-
	About 3m	0	0	0	0	-	-
	About 4m	0	0	0	0	-	-
Bumper	About 2m	0	0	1	1	0%	0%
Total		**0**	**5**	**10**	**15**	**0%**	**33%**

Although there have only been 15 runs from **Sinndar**'s offspring at the Cheltenham Festival, eleven of those runs have taken place in two mile hurdle events, enough to consider whether or not there are any trends on which to base some conclusions. Of those 11 performances, I believe we can discount four of the runs due to the runners being unfancied (three started at 66/1 and one at 200/1). This leaves seven runs to consider, and apart from **Noble Inn** at 20/1, who finished 11th in the 2014 *Fred Winter Juvenile Handicap Hurdle*, and **Hargam** at 16/1, who struggled badly in last season's *Stan James Champion Hurdle Challenge Trophy*, the other five all finished in the first 4 places.

The shortest priced **Sinndar** bred runner to have taken part in the *Fred Winter Juvenile Handicap Hurdle* is **Kazlian**, and the *David Pipe* trained gelding managed to just get into the places in the 2012 renewal when picking up a fourth place paid dividend at odds of 7/1. The progeny have recorded two further 4th place finishes, courtesy of the grey gelding, **Diakali**, who finished fourth on the two occasions that he has run at the Cheltenham Festival. He picked up a place dividend by finishing 4th in the *Vincent O'Brien County Handicap Hurdle* at odds of 25/1 in 2014, having filled the same spot twelve months earlier (but outside the paid places) in the 2013 *JCB Triumph Hurdle*. Two other **Sinndar** bred runners, however, did achieve a place dividend in the *Triumph*. In 2015, *Nicky Henderson* trained the 1st, 2nd and 3rd in the race, with the aforementioned **Hargam**, unsuited to the soft ground, finishing in third. **Hargam** was the second **Sinndar** sired 4 year old to register a 3rd place in the *Triumph*, as six years previously, in the 2009 running, **Mourad** at 14/1, finished behind two greys, runner-up *Walkon* and the winner, *Zaynar*.

It is interesting to note that **Sinndar** is based at the *Aga Khan*'s stud at *Haras National du Lion d'Angers*, and four of the hurdlers already highlighted, **Diakali**, **Mourad**, **Hargam** and **Kazlian** all hail from the *Aga Khan*'s breeding operations. Punters should note that the *Aga Khan's Stud Farms* have an excellent record for producing horses that perform well in two mile novice hurdles at the Cheltenham Festival. A case in point is the 2009 *JCB Triumph Hurdle* mentioned in the previous paragraph, where the *Aga Khan* was the breeder of both the 1st (*Zaynar*) and 3rd (**Mourad**).

Taking the 15 festival runs to date, a reasonable prognosis is that the first **Sinndar** sired Cheltenham Festival winner will be a four year old novice hurdler and a product of the *Aga Khan*'s breeding operations. With that in mind, punters should take a serious interest if they find any **Sinndar** bred runners among the list of entries in Wednesday's *Fred Winter Juvenile Novices' Handicap Hurdle* and also in Friday's opening event, the *JCB Triumph Hurdle*.

Sir Harry Lewis (USA)

Quote from the 2016 Cheltenham Festival Stallion Guide - "In winning the 2007 *Coral Cup*, **Burntoakboy** is the only **Sir Harry Lewis** bred horse to win a Cheltenham Festival race. And with just that one victory to show from 32 efforts in the past decade, the progeny's win strike rate of 3% makes dismal reading."

Sir Harry Lewis (Died as a 25-y-o in 2009)

Race Format	Miles	Won	Placed	Unplaced	Total	Win %	Place %
Hurdles	About 2m	0	0	1	1	0%	0%
	About 2m 4f	1	2	4	7	14%	43%
	About 3m	1	1	6	8	13%	25%
Chases	About 2m	0	0	0	0	-	-
	About 2m 4f	0	0	3	3	0%	0%
	About 3m	0	2	6	8	0%	25%
	About 4m	0	1	3	4	0%	25%
Bumper	About 2m	0	0	2	2	0%	0%
Total		**2**	**6**	**25**	**33**	**6%**	**24%**

In winning the 2016 *Albert Bartlett Novices' Hurdle*, **Unowhatimeanharry** doubled the win strike rate for **Sir Harry Lewis**'s stock at Cheltenham Festivals from 3% to 6%. The only other success for the progeny occurred nine years earlier, when **Burntoakboy** won the 2007 *Coral Cup*. If **Unowhatimeanharry** takes his chance in the 2017 *Sun Bets Stayers' Hurdle*, and follows in the footsteps of three of his predecessors, then I think he will be a solid each way bet. When **Mighty Man**, **Burntoakboy** and **Carole's Legacy** first won or were placed in a Cheltenham Festival race, at the following season's meeting, all three of them gained a place dividend. **Mighty Man**, trained by Henry Daly, hit the frame in two consecutive years in the 2006 and 2007 *Ladbrokes World Hurdle* and **Burntoakboy,** following his 2007 *Coral Cup* success, returned the following year to finish third over 3m1½f in the *Fulke Walwyn Kim Muir Challenge Cup Handicap Chase*. **Carole's Legacy** had a similar profile to **Burntoakboy**, in that having finished runner-up in a 2½ mile hurdle event, (the *2010 David Nicholson Mares' Hurdle*), she also ran in a three mile chase the following year, finishing second and ½ length behind *Bensalem* in the 2011 *Stewart Family Spinal Research Handicap Chase*.

Where the above trio managed to provide a return for punters in two consecutive festivals, the only other two **Sir Harry Lewis** bred horses to be placed at a Cheltenham Festival failed. *Diamond Harry*, third in the 2009 *Ballymore Novices' Hurdle*, disappointed in the following season's *RSA Chase*, when he was pulled up and **Harry The Viking**, who was runner-up in the 2012 *Diamond Jubilee National Hunt Chase*, went down in distance at the next festival when finishing 10th in the 2013 *Fulke Walwyn Kim Muir Challenge Cup Handicap Chase*. At the time of writing, **Unowhatimeanharry** has already laid down his credentials for the festival, when winning both the *Bet365 Long Distance Hurdle* at Newbury in November and Ascot's *JLT Long Walk Hurdle* a week before Christmas. I can't see the Harry Fry trained gelding finishing outside the first three in the 2017 *Sun Bets Stayers' Hurdle*.

Looking deeper into the results of **Sir Harry Lewis** bred festival runners, it is clear that the progeny have had more success over hurdles. Two wins, four places from seventeen hurdle attempts equate to a 35% win and place strike rate. Also, 3 of the 11 that finished out of the frame recorded a top six place. Over fences, the win and place strike rate is 17%, with just three places to show for 18 races over the larger obstacles. Moreover, the next best result outside of the three place positions is seventh, which was achieved by *Thomas Brown* in last season's 2m4½f *Close Brothers Novices' Handicap Chase*.

At Cheltenham Festivals, **Sir Harry Lewis** bred runners are capable of being placed, but find it difficult to win. Despite supporters receiving approximately a return for one in four festival bets, anyone who had backed all of the progeny's festival runners at £1.00 each way over the past decade would be £20.58 poorer. Apart from placing a wager on *Unowhatimeanharry* should he take his chance in the 2017 *Sun Bets Stayers' Hurdle*, I will leave the offspring alone.

Stowaway (GB)

Quote from the 2016 Cheltenham Festival Stallion Guide - "Based on just seven runs, where both victories and one of the place dividends is down to just one horse, we need to be extremely wary of reading too much into the positive statistics highlighted in the table. Nevertheless, all four horses that have represented **Stowaway**'s stock at Cheltenham Festivals have all finished in the top seven places."

Stowaway (Died as a 21-y-o in 2015)							
Race Format	*Miles*	*Won*	*Placed*	*Unplaced*	*Total*	*Win %*	*Place %*
Hurdles	About 2m	1	0	0	1	-	-
	About 2m 4f	0	0	1	1	0%	0%
	About 3m	0	0	1	1	0%	0%
Chases	About 2m	0	1	0	1	0%	100%
	About 2m 4f	0	1	2	3	0%	33%
	About 3m	0	0	1	1	0%	0%
	About 4m	0	0	0	0	-	-
Bumper	About 2m	1	0	0	1	100%	100%
Total		**2**	**2**	**5**	**9**	**22%**	**44%**

If we take all the stallions that were listed in the 2015 and 2016 Cheltenham Festival Stallion Guides, the sire with the lowest number of festival runs that I have featured, is **Stowaway**, who preceding last year's festival meeting, had amassed a grand total of just seven appearances.

The festival performances from **Stowaway**'s progeny are on a downward spiral, starting brilliantly back in 2012 and 2013, just off top quality in 2014, mediocre in 2015, and poor in 2016. I don't believe that this is a trend that will continue, but my albeit previous cautious support for **Stowaway**'s brood is certainly wavering a little.

I will start with the two runs from **Stowaway**'s offspring from last year, both of which took place on the Thursday of the 2016 Cheltenham Festival. In the opening *JLT Novices' Chase*, there were three 4/1 co-favourites in the 9 runner field, with next best being the 6/1 chance, *Outlander*, trained by *Willie Mullins*. *Outlander* was going well enough in 4th place, when he unfortunately fell four fences from home. It was the first time that a **Stowaway** bred runner had failed to complete the course or indeed register a top seven finish in a festival event. The *Charlie Longsdon* trained *Kilcooley* made the ninth festival appearance for **Stowaway**'s stock at odds of 20/1 in the *Ryanair World Hurdle*, and like *Outlander* three races earlier, *Kilcooley* failed to finish the race, being pulled up before two out.

The aforementioned *Outlander* was the first of three **Stowaway** bred runners to take their chance at the 2015 Cheltenham Festival, and in finishing 6th in the *Neptune Investment Management Novices' Hurdle*, not only is *Outlander* the first of **Stowaway**'s offspring to fall at a festival and the first not to gain a top seven finish, he was also the first of the progeny not to register a festival win or place! The other two **Stowaway** sired runners at the 2015 meeting recorded a 7th place in the *Fulke Walwyn Kim Muir Challenge Cup Handicap Chase*, courtesy of 4/1 favourite for the race, *Champagne James*, and a 6th placing with 12/1 chance, *Hidden Cyclone*, in the *Ryanair Chase*. It was *Hidden Cyclone*'s second appearance in the *Ryanair Chase*, his previous run in the 2014 renewal being far more rewarding, when the *John Joseph Hanlon* trained 10/1 chance, finished second and 2¼ lengths behind the winner, *Dynaste*.

In company with **Hidden Cyclone**, the other **Stowaway** bred runner to record a festival place position, is the *Willie Mullins* trained, **Champagne Fever**, who just missed out on a hat-trick of Cheltenham Festival victories in the 2014 *Racing Post Arkle Challenge Trophy Chase*. Having led all the way in the race, the 11/4 favourite was eventually beaten by a head in the dying strides, by the strong finishing 33/1 outsider, *Western Warhorse*.

Champagne Fever, owned by *Susannah Ricci*, was the first of **Stowaway**'s offspring to line up in a festival event, when entered for the 2012 *Weatherbys Champion Bumper*. Ridden by the trainer's son, *Patrick Mullins*, the grey gelding led from start to finish, winning the race at the rewarding odds of 16/1. The following season, **Champagne Fever** made it two wins from two in festival events when having made all in the *William Hill Supreme Novices' Hurdle*, he was overtaken at the last hurdle by the 15/8 favourite, *My Tent Or Yours*, only to rally gamely on the run in to beat the market leader by half a length.

With regard to the 44% win and place strike rate showing in **Stowaway**'s festival performance table above, there is no denying that the star of the show is **Champagne Fever**, responsible for 75% of the progeny's win and place positions to date. And, it is very unfortunate that the horse hasn't been seen at Cheltenham since he was beaten in the *Arkle* in March 2014. **Champagne Fever** was fully expected to run in the 2015 *Betway Queen Mother Champion Chase*, when he was declared a non-runner on the morning of the race having suffered a small injury in transit when travelling to Cheltenham from Ireland. Having bypassed Cheltenham, *Willie Mullins* entered **Champagne Fever** in two Grade 1 contests in April 2015, but the grey gelding was off the boil and finished outside the places in both the *Betfred Melling Chase* at *Aintree* and also the *Boylesports Champion Chase* at *Punchestown*. **Champagne Fever**'s next race occurred 576 days later in November 2016, when the horse narrowly defeated the 2014 *Gold Cup* winner, *Lord Windermere*, in a listed chase event at *Thurles*. It will be great if **Champagne Fever** is fit enough to make it to the Cheltenham Festival this spring, and for that matter, it would be good to see *Lord Windermere* make an appearance too.

In summary, **Stowaway**'s brood made a blistering start in their early festival appearances, but in the past two years, there have been five rather uninspiring runs from the offspring. With that in mind, I am rather undecided on the likely success or otherwise of **Stowaway** sired runners at the 2017 Cheltenham Festival. My hunch is that, over time, the progeny will provide us with further festival successes, but at this juncture, I will maintain a watching brief and see what the position is when **Stowaway**'s stock have had a few more festival runs under their belt.

Turgeon (USA)

Quote from the 2016 Cheltenham Festival Stallion Guide - *"Chapoturgeon* stands alone twice. First, he is the only **Turgeon** sired winner of a Cheltenham Festival race, having won the *Jewson Novices' Handicap Chase* in 2009. Secondly, in a total of 17 festival chase runs by the progeny in the past ten years, he is the only one to register a finishing position outside of the top 8 places."

Turgeon (31-y-o)

Race Format	Miles	Won	Placed	Unplaced	Total	Win %	Place %
	About 2m	0	0	2	2	0%	0%
Hurdles	About 2m 4f	0	0	2	2	0%	0%
	About 3m	0	0	0	0	-	-
	About 2m	0	0	0	0	-	-
	About 2m 4f	1	2	1	4	25%	75%
Chases	About 3m	0	5	9	14	0%	36%
	About 4m	0	0	0	0	-	-
Bumper	About 2m	0	0	1	1	0%	0%
Total		**1**	**7**	**15**	**23**	**4%**	**35%**

I will kick off this section with **Chapoturgeon**, as not only is the grey gelding highlighted in the quote at the top of the page, but he was also one of just two **Turgeon** sired horses who ran at the 2016 Cheltenham Festival. In looking at all of **Turgeon**'s offspring to have run at Cheltenham Festivals, **Chapoturgeon** is rather good at being unique on a number of fronts. As mentioned in the 2016 Stallion Guide, he stands alone as the only one of **Turgeon**'s progeny to have won a Cheltenham Festival race. He is also the only **Turgeon** bred runner to have been pulled up whilst contesting a festival chase event, this being the 2013 *CGA Foxhunter Chase Challenge Cup*, although to be fair, there had been an avalanche of rain that race day, making it tough going for all the runners and hence only 4 of the 23 who set out actually completed the race. As an aside, there has only been one other occasion where a **Turgeon** sired runner has been pulled up, this being the 500/1 rank outsider, **Turnium**, who was pulled up before the last in the 2006 *Smurfit Kappa Champion Hurdle Challenge Trophy*. Finally, we come to last year's Cheltenham meeting, when **Chapoturgeon** managed to achieve two more firsts. Being a 12 year old, in last year's *St. James's Place Foxhunter Chase Challenge Cup*, he became the oldest of all of **Turgeon**'s progeny to have lined up in a Cheltenham Festival race. In the event itself, **Chapoturgeon** was making some headway three out, albeit making no real impression on the leaders, when he fell two fences from home. This is the only occurrence of **Turgeon**'s stock falling in a festival race in a total of 31 attempts!

Interestingly, the 2016 Cheltenham Festival also featured a very first appearance for **Turgeon**'s progeny in the *Weatherbys Champion Bumper*, when the *Katie Walsh* ridden, **Turcagua**, one of seven *Willie Mullins* trained entrants in the race, finished 15th at odds of 33/1.

The speciality of **Turgeon** sired runners is encouraging runs in chase events without actually winning, as evidenced by the past decade's 16 from 18 top eight finishes, eight of which resulted in a win or place dividend. For the record, if one had backed all eighteen of **Turgeon**'s progeny over fences in the past decade, it would have produced a small profit of £1.75 to a £1.00 each way stake. As for the Cheltenham Festival hurdle events, **Turgeon**'s offspring have only been engaged in four races within the past decade, with the highest finishing position being ninth.

In conclusion, for horses sired by **Turgeon**, the recommendation is straightforward. Ignore the offspring in hurdle events and back them each way over fences.

Turtle Island (IRE)

Quote from the 2016 Cheltenham Festival Stallion Guide - "Over the past 10 festivals, if one had backed every **Turtle Island** sired runner each way, where the horse had an SP under 20/1, it would have produced a £6.95 profit to a £1.00 stake. If one includes Cheltenham Festivals pre-2006, and therefore *Scolardy*'s 16/1 victory, then the resulting profit is £24.15 to a £1.00 each way stake."

Turtle Island (26-y-o)

Race Format	Miles	Won	Placed	Unplaced	Total	Win %	Place %
	About 2m	0	0	1	1	0%	0%
Hurdles	About 2m 4f	0	1	4	5	0%	20%
	About 3m	0	1	3	4	0%	25%
	About 2m	0	0	1	1	0%	0%
	About 2m 4f	0	0	2	2	0%	0%
Chases	About 3m	1	0	3	4	25%	25%
	About 4m	0	0	4	4	0%	0%
Bumper	About 2m	0	0	3	3	0%	0%
Total		**1**	**2**	**21**	**24**	**4%**	**13%**

One can probably skip through this commentary on how well **Turtle Island**'s offspring have performed at Cheltenham Festivals. First, I don't anticipate there being many runners from the progeny at the 2017 Festival, and secondly, if you do find a **Turtle Island** sired runner among this year's entries, if the starting price is 20/1 or greater, then you can safely ignore it.

As it stands, in the past decade, 19 of the 24 **Turtle Island** bred runners have started at an SP of 20/1 or greater, of which 14 were sent off at odds of 33/1 plus. As one would expect, the majority of these **Turtle Island** bred outsiders finished well down the field, with just three runs resulting in a top six finish, two of which were secured seven years apart by *Shoreacres*. In 2015, he finished 6th in the *St. James's Place Foxhunter Chase Challenge Cup* at odds of 40/1. The gelding's odds were double that seven years earlier, when in the 2008 *Weatherbys Champion Bumper*, *Shoreacres* ran well to secure 4th position at odds of 80/1. The only other outsider to reach a top six place was *Our Island* at 50/1, when he finished fifth in the 2013 *John Oaksey National Hunt Chase*. So, when it came to the 2016 Cheltenham Festival meeting, it was no surprise that, at odds of 66/1, the sole representative of **Turtle's Island**'s stock, failed to trouble the judge. The horse was *Warrantor*, who having blundered four out causing the saddle to slip and his rider, *Mr Joshua Newman*, to lose his irons, was pulled up in the *146th Year of the National Hunt Chase Challenge Cup*.

One may want to know about the five runs from **Turtle Island**'s offspring where the odds were below 20/1? The sole winner from 24 runs in the past decade is courtesy of *Bensalem*, trained by *Alan King*, who won the 2011 *Stewart Family Spinal Research Handicap* Chase over three miles at odds of 5/1. He also ran in the same race the previous season, albeit that the race in 2010 was sponsored by *William Hill (The William Hill Trophy Handicap Chase)*. His price on this occasion was 6/1 and as the race developed in earnest, it certainly appeared as if he would have a major say in the finish. Having made steady headway at the 15th, he was travelling well and tracking the leaders when he fell two out.

Of the other three **Turtle Island** bred runners who started at a price of below 20/1, two of them secured a place dividend. In 2008, the *Charles Byrnes* trained **Liskennett**, ran well to take the runner-up spot at a price of 16/1 in the *Albert Bartlett Novices' Hurdle* over three miles. Two years later, **Clova Island**, trained by *Philip Hobbs* finished third at 14/1 in the *Martin Pipe Conditional Jockeys' Handicap Hurdle*. For the record, pre-2005, there were two more runners sired by **Turtle Island** who started at below 20/1 and they both ran in the 2002 *JCB Triumph Hurdle*. **Scolardy**, won the race at 16/1, whilst **Turtleback** who also started at 16/1, finished sixth. So, in summary, there have been seven festival occasions in total when the market has determined an SP of less than 20/1 for a **Turtle Island** bred runner. And those runners have generally performed well and produced two wins, two places, a sixth, and another who looked certain to at least place if not win, before falling two out. To complete the picture, the seventh shorter priced runner was our old friend **Shoreacres** again, who this time at just 6/1, could only manage 14th in the 2011 *Johnny Henderson Grand Annual Chase Challenge Cup*.

Despite the poor figures shown in the above table, the underlying reality is that the more fancied of **Turtle Island**'s progeny, towards the front of the betting market, perform creditably at Cheltenham Festivals, and come this spring, I will not discount any **Turtle Island** bred runners from my calculations should they be racing at odds shorter than 20/1.

Voix Du Nord (FR)

Quote from the 2016 Cheltenham Festival Stallion Guide - "It is unrealistic to compile any trends with so few runs, but with four of the progeny having achieved a top six position, in general, I suggest that the offspring have performed reasonably well."

Voix Du Nord (Died as a 12-y-o in 2013)

Race Format	Miles	Won	Placed	Unplaced	Total	Win %	Place %
	About 2m	0	1	3	4	0%	25%
Hurdles	About 2m 4f	1	0	2	3	33%	33%
	About 3m	0	1	2	3	0%	33%
	About 2m	0	0	2	2	0%	0%
Chases	About 2m 4f	1	0	5	6	17%	17%
	About 3m	0	0	0	0	-	-
	About 4m	0	0	0	0	-	-
Bumper	About 2m	0	0	0	0	-	-
Total		**2**	**2**	**14**	**18**	**11%**	**22%**

Before last year, only seven **Voix Du Nord** bred horses had been at a Cheltenham Festival making up a total of eleven festival runs for the progeny. With so little information to go on, it was difficult to make any sound conclusions, but with eight of the eleven runs resulting in a top 8 finish, including one win and two places, I considered the early signs for the offspring to be encouraging. The seven runs from **Voix Du Nord**'s stock at the 2017 Cheltenham Festival have reinforced that view, and I am now very much convinced that **Voix Du Nord**'s progeny are well worth supporting.

It may come as a surprise to many that following last year's meeting, I am even more positive about the chances of the offspring, especially when one considers that of the seven runners who set out in their respective races last year, only three of them managed to complete the course. Freakishly, at the 2017 Cheltenham Festival, two **Voix Du Nord** bred runners fell and another couple unseated their rider. The progeny were blemish free prior to last year's meeting with all eleven runners having stayed on their feet.

It is important to analyse the four races in which horse and jockey parted company, as it will help to justify my confidence in supporting **Voix Du Nord**'s stock at future festivals. In the second race of the festival, the *Racing Post Arkle Challenge Trophy Chase*, *Douvan* only had six competitors. I guess that the six who took him on were hoping that the *Willie Mullins* trained favourite would blunder and lose his jockey, *Ruby Walsh*, at one of the 13 fences. It didn't happen of course, and the 1/4 odds-on shot won comfortably. One horse that did blunder, however, and unseat his rider two fences from home, was the **Voix Du Nord** sired, *Vaniteux*, who lined up in the race as the 8/1 second favourite. Although *Vaniteux* was starting to challenge rounding the home turn, *Douvan* was never in any danger as he powered away, and the only unknown was which of his closest pursuers, *Vaniteux* or *Sizing John*, would follow him home. *Vaniteux* was 1½ lengths behind *Douvan* and under pressure when he blundered and unseated *Nico De Boinville* two out, leaving *Sizing John* (9/1) to take the runner-up spot for forecast backers.

The following day, in the *Fred Winter Juvenile Handicap Hurdle*, **Voix Du Reve** was making headway three from home, travelling well and mounting a strong challenge when falling at the last. I've watched the race replay on a number of occasions, and although one can rarely be certain as to the likely outcome of a contest had a horse not fallen, in my view, *Voix Du Reve* would have won the race, especially as the **Voix Du Nord** bred 14/1 chance would have been assisted in the run to the line by the hugely experienced *Ruby Walsh*.

On the Thursday of last year's meeting, although travelling comfortably enough at the time in ninth place, no conclusions can be drawn from the fall of the *Paul Nicholls* trained, **Vibrato Valtat**, in the *Ryanair Chase*. The 33/1 outsider parted company with jockey, *Sam Twiston-Davies*, four from home.

Having seen a **Voix Du Nord** sired horse lose his jockey on each of the first three days of the 2017 Cheltenham Festival, **Bachasson** made it 4 out of 4 on the final day of the meeting, when he unseated jockey *Patrick Mullins* at the final hurdle in the *Albert Bartlett Novices' Hurdle*. The 28/1 shot was in the process of running a respectable race, disputing 5th and about six lengths off the pace, before he blundered at the last. Had **Bachasson** managed to stay on his feet, then the most likely outcome would have been a top six finish, albeit very doubtful that he would have troubled the front three.

Of the three **Voix Du Nord** bred festival entries who managed to complete their races, there were two acceptable enough performances from two of the runners to deliver a top 8 finish and a victory from an odds-on favourite in the *OLBG Mares' Hurdle*. This Grade 1 race open to mares aged four years or older and registered as the *David Nicholson Mares' Hurdle Race*, has been dominated by trainer *Willie Mullins*. The first running of the event took place in 2008, when *Whiteoak* won the race for trainer *Donald McCain*. Ever since then, the race has belonged to the *Willie Mullins* yard, with six consecutive wins for the brilliant *Quevega* from 2009 through to 2014, followed by victories for *Glens Melody* in 2015 and last year, the **Voix Du Nord** sired, **Vroum Vroum Mag**. *Ruby Walsh* was in command on **Vroum Vroum Mag** heading towards the last hurdle, and the only danger was a repeat of the previous year's disaster, when *Annie Power*, his odds-on shot in the 2015 renewal, fell at the last flight when 4 lengths clear. Happily for *Ruby Walsh*, there was to be no recurrence, and **Vroum Vroum Mag**, the 4/6 favourite, won stylishly.

The previous festival victory registered against **Voix Du Nord**'s progeny was achieved by **Taquin Du Seuil**. He was the very first and only runner for the progeny at the 2013 Cheltenham Festival, when he finished 6th in the *Neptune Investment Management Novices' Hurdle*. The following season, **Taquin Du Seuil** secured the first festival victory for **Voix Du Nord**'s offspring, when *A P McCoy* rode the horse to victory in the *JLT Novices' Chase* at odds of 7/1. For the past two seasons, the *Jonjo O'Neill* trained gelding has taken part in the *Ryanair Chase*, In 2015, he finished down the field after blundering 4 from home and in last year's renewal, although performing slightly better, he never threatened the leaders and eventually came in sixth.

Out of the 18 runs from **Voix Du Nord**'s stock, the two place positions have occurred over hurdles. The previously mentioned **Vaniteux** (11/1), was one of two runners from the *Nicky Henderson* stable in the 2014 *Sky Bet Supreme Novices' Hurdle* when finishing 3rd at the heels of stablemate *Josses Hill*, who took the runner-up spot behind easy winner and 6/4 favourite, *Vautour*. And in the 2015 *Pertemps Network Final*, the David Pipe trained **Unique de Cotte** (14/1) ran well to finish runner-up when beaten by the strong finishing *Call The Cops*.

If one had placed a £1.00 each-way bet on all 18 festival runs of **Voix Du Nord**'s offspring, the outcome would have been a loss of £15.10. Despite this, in looking at the overall record of the progeny, I think a profit for punters is just around the corner. In those 18 runs, there have been two wins and two places, and of the other ten runners who were unplaced but managed to stay on their feet, only one of them has failed to achieve a top ten placing. Furthermore, if we look at the four **Voix Du Nord** sired horses who unseated their riders or fell, the very strong likelihood is that all of them would have attained a top ten finish had they stayed on their feet, with a possibility of a runner-up spot from *Vaniteux*, and in my opinion, a potential 3rd victory for the progeny in the shape of *Voix Du Reve*.

Albeit there are only 18 festival performances on which to base any opinion, I will stick my neck out and suggest that there is a distinct possibility that punters will make a profit by backing **Voix Du Nord**'s offspring at the 2017 Cheltenham Festival.

Westerner (GB)

Quote from the 2016 Cheltenham Festival Stallion Guide - "With two victories and three place dividends from just 18 festival runs, the future looks bright for this young 17 year old stallion. And supporters of **Westerner**'s offspring have been rewarded with some big price festival successes."

Westerner (18-y-o)

Race Format	Miles	Won	Placed	Unplaced	Total	Win %	Place %
	About 2m	0	1	2	3	0%	33%
Hurdles	About 2m 4f	0	1	4	5	0%	20%
	About 3m	1	1	8	10	10%	20%
	About 2m	2	0	0	2	100%	100%
Chases	About 2m 4f	1	0	4	5	20%	20%
	About 3m	0	0	2	2	0%	0%
	About 4m	0	0	1	1	0%	0%
Bumper	About 2m	0	0	2	2	0%	0%
Total		**4**	**3**	**23**	**30**	**13%**	**23%**

Punters, who like to back favourites and short price runners at Cheltenham Festivals, would have been delighted with the 2016 meeting. Last year, eleven favourites won their races, whereas in the previous five festivals, the number of favourites to win ranged between 6 and 9. And in the 28 races last season, just two of the festival winners had odds of 16/1 or more. Between 2011 and 2015 with one less race (27 contests in total), for all five years, there were at least six winners with an SP of 16/1 or greater.

Against the above backdrop, where the Winners Enclosure at last year's Cheltenham Festival was largely devoid of winning outsiders, my recommendation to support **Westerner**'s offspring, especially because of the recent history of big price **Westerner** sired winners, was potentially going to be wide of the mark. Nevertheless, do you know which stallion sired the two biggest priced winners at the 2016 Cheltenham Festival? You've guessed it, **Westerner**!

It is remarkable that we had to wait for the 28th and final race of the 2016 Cheltenham Festival, before we witnessed a winner with an SP of greater than 16/1. *Solar Impulse*, ridden by *Sam Twiston-Davies*, led approaching the last fence and ran on strongly to beat *Dandridge* by 3¾ lengths in the *Johnny Henderson Grand Annual Chase Challenge Cup*. Trained by *Paul Nicholls*, the **Westerner** sired winner rewarded supporters handsomely by returning a starting price of 28/1. It was the second time that **Westerner**'s offspring had had a runner in a Cheltenham Festival two mile chase event. On the first occasion, in the 2014 *Arkle*, **Western Warhorse** (33/1), managed to beat the *Willie Mullins* trained favourite *Champagne Fever*, by a head. It was a fantastic ride by *Tom Scudamore*, who managed to galvanise **Western Warhorse** to deliver a strong run under pressure from the last, before just getting the better of *Ruby Walsh*'s mount in the final stride. Hence, **Westerner** bred runners have a 100% success record in Cheltenham Festival 2m chases, albeit only two runs so far!

The next biggest priced winner at last year's festival occurred in the *Brown Advisory & Merriebelle Stable Plate*, run over a distance of 2m5f. Two of **Westerner**'s offspring were entered in the race, the

11/2 joint favourite, *Stiletto*, who fell at the third fence and the *Bryan Cooper* ridden 16/1 shot, *Empire Of Dirt*, who was well in command after leading two out, and won the race comfortably.

The victories of *Empire of Dirt* and *Solar Impulse* double the number of festival winners for **Westerner**'s stock to four, producing an impressive win strike rate for the progeny of 13%. Of even more significance is the huge profit to be gained in backing the stallion's festival entries, which stands at a mammoth £65.00 if one had placed a £1.00 win bet on all 30 of **Westerner** sired festival runners to date.

The shortest priced festival winner of **Westerner**'s offspring is *Cole Harden*, who was victorious in the 2015 *Ladbrokes World Hurdle* at odds of 14/1. It was a well-deserved and first ever Cheltenham Festival victory for both the trainer, *Warren Greatrex*, and jockey, *Gavin Sheehan*.

Supporters of **Westerner**'s offspring have enjoyed sizable profits at previous festival meetings and I'm convinced the winners will keep on coming for this 18 year old stallion. Racking up four victories and three place dividends, at odds of between 9/1 and 33/1, from just 30 festival runners, is simply phenomenal.

Winged Love (IRE)

Quote from the 2016 Cheltenham Festival Stallion Guide - "I suggested that punters may have a better chance of success in the festival's three mile chases. And as it turns out, the advice wasn't misplaced, when in the *Fulke Walwyn Kim Muir Challenge Cup Handicap Chase*, *Nina Carberry* rode the *Gordon Elliott* trained, **Bless The Wings**, into the runner-up spot at the rewarding odds of 28/1."

Race Format	Miles	Won	Placed	Unplaced	Total	Win %	Place %
				Winged Love (Died as a 23-y-o in 2015)			
	About 2m	0	1	2	3	0%	33%
Hurdles	About 2m 4f	0	0	0	0	-	-
	About 3m	0	0	5	5	0%	0%
	About 2m	0	1	4	5	0%	20%
Chases	About 2m 4f	1	1	8	10	10%	20%
	About 3m	1	1	8	10	10%	20%
	About 4m	0	2	5	7	0%	29%
Bumper	About 2m	0	0	1	1	0%	0%
Total		**2**	**6**	**33**	**41**	**5%**	**20%**

Over the past decade, 20 of **Winged Love's** offspring have been engaged in 41 races at Cheltenham Festivals. Sixteen of the **Winged Love** sired horses have failed to provide any sort of return for festival bets placed on them. The other four of the progeny, however, are responsible for all eight win and place positions, having a win or a place to their name on two of their festival outings.

At the 2016 Cheltenham Festival, eight runners represented **Winged Love's** stock, and in hindsight, provided **Bless The Wings** was to follow the example set by **Bostons Angel, Hunt Ball** and **Josses Hill**, it was glaringly obvious that **Bless The Wings** would finish in the first three places in the *Glenfarclas Chase*. When it comes to **Winged Love's** stock, here is the rule for punters. Should a horse sired by **Winged Love** win or be placed at a Cheltenham Festival for the first time in its career, place a very large each way bet on the same horse the next time that it appears in a festival race! Admittedly this is a peculiar coincidence, but the truth is that when **Bostons Angel, Hunt Ball, Josses Hill** and now **Bless The Wings** all managed to win or be placed in a festival race, the very next time they lined up in a Cheltenham Festival contest, all four of them gained a place dividend.

The *Jessica Harrington* trained, **Bostons Angel**, was the first of **Winged Love's** progeny to win a festival race, when landing the Grade 1 *RSA Chase* in 2011 at odds of 16/1. Having lost form afterwards, **Bostons Angel** missed the 2012 festival, but returned in 2013 to tackle Cheltenham's Cross Country course and was rewarded with a place dividend by finishing 4th in the *Glenfarclas Handicap Chase*. **Hunt Ball**, who between November 2011 and February 2012 enjoyed a spectacular rise through the handicap ranks, became the progeny's second festival winner. In just four months, the horse won six races and climbed from a mark of 69 to 142, before being raised another 12 pounds as a result of his Cheltenham Festival victory in the listed 2012 *Pulteney Land Investments Novices' Handicap* over 2½ miles. At the following season's meeting, **Hunt Ball's** trainer, *Kieran Burke*, entered him in the Grade 3 *Byrne Group Plate*, and the horse secured a fourth place dividend in what was another satisfying performance from the horse. In 2015, **Josses Hill** was tackling the festival for a second time, following on from his runner-up spot in the 2014 *Sky Bet Supreme Novices' Hurdle*. Running over two miles again, this time over the larger obstacles in the *Racing Post*

Arkle Challenge Trophy Chase, the *Nicky Henderson* trained gelding did not disappoint supporters, staying on to finish 3rd at odds of 12/1.

When trained by *Alan King* at *Barbury Castle*, **Bless The Wings** raced in festival races between 2012 and 2014, but was rather disappointing in all three appearances when finishing down the field on every occasion. At the 2015 festival, having moved to *Gordon Elliott's* yard, the now ten year old wasn't especially fancied to trouble the leaders when he lined up in the *Fulke Walwyn Kim Muir Challenge Cup Handicap Chase*. However, the change of scenery had clearly had an effect, as *Nina Carberry* rode **Bless The Wings** into the runner-up spot at the rewarding odds of 28/1. At the 2016 Cheltenham Festival, **Bless The Wings** returned to line up in the cross country *Glenfarclas Chase*. The horse had already raced over course and distance in the November and December of 2015, where both races had been won by the *Enda Bolger* trained, *Josies Orders*. **Bless The Wings** finished third and 6 lengths behind the winner in November, and fourth and more than 25 lengths behind the same horse a month later. When it came to the festival race, once again **Bless The Wings** was unfancied, despite being ridden by the excellent amateur jockey, *Jamie Codd*. As it turned out, the result was not too different to what had happened over course and distance twice previously, although this time **Bless The Wings**, at 33/1, managed to finish just 1¼ lengths away from the favourite, *Josies Orders*. On the day, both horses finished 2nd and 3rd, behind the *Aidan Coleman* ridden, *Any Currency*. Five months later, however, *Any Currency* was disqualified due to a positive post-race drugs test, thereby *Josies Orders* being promoted to first and **Bless The Wings** to second.

In the 2016 Cheltenham Festival Stallion Guide, I pointed out that statistically, three mile chases stood out as the most likely category where punters could be rewarded in backing **Winged Love**'s stock. And in last season's 3m 2f *Fulke Walwyn Kim Muir Challenge Cup Handicap Chase*, two of the progeny were listed amongst the 22 runners, both having a starting price of 33/1. **Perfect Candidate**, never got into the race and finished tenth, but **Lost Legend**, ridden by *Mr S Clements*, was just beginning to make ground and looking as if he may get involved towards the business end of the race, when he unfortunately fell four from home. As it stands today, **Winged Love**'s offspring has delivered a top six finish in 6 of the 10 three mile festival chases that have been contested, a hit rate that is notably better than the other race categories. To emphasise the point further, if we omit the results attained by **Bostons Angel, Hunt Ball, Josses Hill** and **Bless The Wings**, then the statistics within the 3m chase category still hold up well with 4 top six finishes from a total of 8 races. In comparison, if we take all the other race categories combined over the past 10 years, we end up with a total of 17 races where only once has a **Winged Love** sired runner achieved a top six finish, and that was a 6th placing in a race where only 8 horses participated!

For the 2017 Cheltenham Festival, if *Jonjo O'Neill* enters **Lost Legend** in a race, then I may place a small wager on him, based upon his two runs at the festival to date, these being a respectable sixth place in the 2015 *Ultima Business Solutions Handicap Chase* followed by his promising run, before falling four from home, in last year's *Fulke Walwyn Kim Muir Challenge Cup Handicap Chase*. For all other **Winged Love** sired runners that turn up in March, I will avoid them. Perhaps there is a marginal case to support the progeny in the festival's three mile chases, but when it comes to the other race categories, my strong recommendation is to leave well alone.

Incidentally, should a **Winged Love** sired runner manage a win or place at the 2017 festival, my recommendation will be very easy in next year's Cheltenham Festival Stallion Guide. If the same horse is entered at the 2018 festival, then place a large each way bet on it!

Index Table by Stallion

This table shows the BHA Official Ratings (as of January 2017) for National Hunt horses listed from the 2015/16 season onwards. Only horses that were showing an official rating of 130 or greater in January 2017 are listed. Index is in alphabetical order and only for stallions listed within this Guide.

Sire	Horse	Age	Sex	Official Rating as of January 2017
Al Namix	Abricot De L'Oasis	7	g	131
Al Namix	Baby Mix	9	g	141
Al Namix	Ballyhill	6	g	136
Al Namix	Mr Mix	6	g	145
Al Namix	Petit Mouchoir	6	g	162
Al Namix	Saphir Du Rheu	8	g	154
Alflora	Al Alfa	10	g	131
Alflora	Alfie Spinner	12	g	135
Alflora	Chase The Spud	9	g	132
Alflora	Cultivator	6	g	140
Alflora	Dare To Endeavour	10	g	130
Alflora	Fine Rightly	9	g	150
Alflora	Pearlysteps	14	g	132
Alflora	Potters Cross	10	g	139
Alflora	Smooth Stepper	8	g	134
Alflora	Wishfull Thinking	14	g	162
Assessor	Anibale Fly	7	g	148
Assessor	Coo Star Sivola	5	g	134
Assessor	Reve De Sivola	12	g	153
Astarabad	Jolly's Cracked It	8	g	144
Astarabad	Missy Tata	5	m	145
Astarabad	Sirabad	7	g	134
Astarabad	Traffic Fluide	7	g	165
Astarabad	Whisper	9	g	159
Authorized	Altruism	7	g	140
Authorized	Automated	6	g	136
Authorized	Beltor	6	g	135
Authorized	Boite	7	g	142
Authorized	Craggaknock	6	g	135
Authorized	El Namoose	8	g	141
Authorized	Ennistown	7	g	140
Authorized	Nichols Canyon	7	g	160
Authorized	Rejaah	5	m	136
Authorized	Shwaiman	7	g	130
Authorized	Sternrubin	6	g	143
Authorized	Tiger Roll	7	g	145
Authorized	Totalize	8	g	144
Authorized	Zamdy Man	7	g	140
Authorized	Zubayr	5	g	141
Ballingarry	Aubusson	8	g	145
Ballingarry	Balgarry	10	g	136
Ballingarry	Charlemar	5	g	135
Ballingarry	Diego Du Charmil	5	g	140
Ballingarry	Full Shift	8	g	135

Sire	Horse	Age	Sex	Official Rating as of January 2017
Ballingarry	Katgary	7	g	137
Ballingarry	Samingarry	10	g	134
Beneficial	A Genie In Abottle	6	g	142
Beneficial	Annacotty	9	g	154
Beneficial	Another Bill	7	g	130
Beneficial	Benbens	12	g	140
Beneficial	Bennys Mist	11	g	139
Beneficial	Bentelimar	8	g	138
Beneficial	Benvolio	10	g	145
Beneficial	Big Chief Benny	6	g	133
Beneficial	Bonny Kate	7	m	138
Beneficial	Capard King	8	g	135
Beneficial	Cloonacool	8	g	140
Beneficial	Coillte Lass	6	m	137
Beneficial	Colms Dream	8	g	142
Beneficial	De Plotting Shed	7	g	150
Beneficial	Eastlake	11	g	154
Beneficial	Fingeronotheswitch	7	g	137
Beneficial	Forever Field	7	g	135
Beneficial	Howlongisafoot	8	g	134
Beneficial	Hurricane Ben	8	g	133
Beneficial	It's A Gimme	10	g	137
Beneficial	Jetstream Jack	7	g	140
Beneficial	Katie T	8	m	139
Beneficial	Kilcrea Vale	7	g	142
Beneficial	Last Encounter	7	g	130
Beneficial	Lift The Latch	7	g	141
Beneficial	Living Next Door	11	g	145
Beneficial	Mala Beach	9	g	150
Beneficial	Marlbrook	9	g	143
Beneficial	Monksland	10	g	148
Beneficial	More Of That	9	g	167
Beneficial	Mount Colah	11	g	143
Beneficial	One Term	10	g	135
Beneficial	Phobiaphiliac	6	g	132
Beneficial	Rathnure Rebel	7	g	140
Beneficial	Realt Mor	12	g	138
Beneficial	Red Devil Lads	8	g	134
Beneficial	Ruben Cotter	11	g	139
Beneficial	Salubrious	10	g	148
Beneficial	Scotchtown	5	g	135
Beneficial	Sego Success	9	g	138
Beneficial	Storm Of Swords	9	g	130
Beneficial	Ten Times Better	7	m	130
Beneficial	Upswing	9	g	132
Beneficial	Yesyoucan	12	g	134
Cape Cross	Cardinal Walter	8	g	135
Cape Cross	Devilment	6	g	146
Cape Cross	Jalingo	6	g	130
Cape Cross	Leoncavallo	5	g	143

Sire	Horse	Age	Sex	Official Rating as of January 2017
Cape Cross	Ruacana	8	g	137
Cape Cross	Sky Khan	8	g	132
Cape Cross	Wakea	6	g	143
Definite Article	Ballybogey	11	g	130
Definite Article	Cailin Annamh	9	m	145
Definite Article	Definite Outcome	8	g	132
Definite Article	Definitly Red	8	g	149
Definite Article	Fine Article	8	g	138
Definite Article	Heathfield	10	g	130
Definite Article	Macnicholson	8	g	136
Definite Article	Mountain King	8	g	133
Definite Article	Pingshou	7	g	133
Definite Article	Sizing Platinum	9	g	141
Definite Article	Some Article	9	g	132
Definite Article	The Horsechesnut	9	g	130
Dom Alco	Al Co	12	g	139
Dom Alco	Al Ferof	12	g	162
Dom Alco	Antartica De Thaix	7	m	132
Dom Alco	Arpege D'Alene	7	g	149
Dom Alco	Baron Alco	6	g	143
Dom Alco	Gevrey Chambertin	9	g	145
Dom Alco	Roalco De Farges	12	g	130
Dom Alco	Silviniaco Conti	11	g	161
Dom Alco	Sire Collonges	11	g	137
Dom Alco	Turban	10	g	133
Dom Alco	Unioniste	9	g	141
Dom Alco	Valco De Touzaine	8	g	140
Dom Alco	Vicente	8	g	149
Dom Alco	Vivaldi Collonges	8	g	148
Dr Massini	Doctor Phoenix	9	g	141
Dr Massini	Dr Mikey	8	g	136
Dr Massini	Fair Dilemma	12	g	138
Dr Massini	Fear Glic	11	g	130
Dr Massini	Forgotten Gold	11	g	143
Dr Massini	Foxtail Hill	8	g	133
Dr Massini	Indian Castle	9	g	131
Dr Massini	Justforjames	8	g	130
Dr Massini	Massini's Trap	8	g	132
Dr Massini	Rocky Creek	11	g	148
Dr Massini	Sound Investment	9	g	160
Dr Massini	Three Faces West	9	g	147
Flemensfirth	Abolitionist	9	g	135
Flemensfirth	Andy Kelly	8	g	130
Flemensfirth	Aqua Dude	7	g	136
Flemensfirth	Arctic Skipper	8	g	148
Flemensfirth	Beast Of Burden	8	g	131
Flemensfirth	Beg To Differ	7	g	139
Flemensfirth	Burn And Turn	11	m	138
Flemensfirth	Closing Ceremony	8	g	142
Flemensfirth	Coney Island	6	g	152

Sire	Horse	Age	Sex	Official Rating as of January 2017
Flemensfirth	Emily Gray	9	m	148
Flemensfirth	Emperor's Choice	10	g	135
Flemensfirth	Enjoy Responsibly	8	g	130
Flemensfirth	Father Edward	8	g	134
Flemensfirth	Firth Of The Clyde	12	g	145
Flemensfirth	Flaming Dawn	9	g	130
Flemensfirth	Flemenstar	12	g	155
Flemensfirth	Gala Ball	7	g	143
Flemensfirth	Hester Flemen	9	m	132
Flemensfirth	Highland Lodge	11	g	140
Flemensfirth	Hunters Hoof	8	g	130
Flemensfirth	Invitation Only	6	g	138
Flemensfirth	Jennies Jewel	10	m	147
Flemensfirth	Jett	6	g	132
Flemensfirth	Johnny Og	8	g	136
Flemensfirth	Killer Miller	8	g	136
Flemensfirth	Kimberlite Candy	5	g	134
Flemensfirth	Kk Lexion	6	g	135
Flemensfirth	Knockgraffon	7	g	144
Flemensfirth	Meister Eckhart	11	g	140
Flemensfirth	Minella Daddy	7	g	145
Flemensfirth	Mister Spingsprong	10	g	139
Flemensfirth	Montoya's Son	12	g	131
Flemensfirth	Mosspark	9	g	135
Flemensfirth	Noble Endeavor	8	g	153
Flemensfirth	O O Seven	7	g	152
Flemensfirth	One Track Mind	7	g	158
Flemensfirth	Padge	8	g	143
Flemensfirth	Preseli Rock	7	g	130
Flemensfirth	Prince Of Scars	7	g	159
Flemensfirth	Robinsfirth	8	g	140
Flemensfirth	Rock On The Moor	9	m	140
Flemensfirth	Sharpasaknife	7	g	131
Flemensfirth	Sizing Codelco	8	g	141
Flemensfirth	Sizing Gold	10	g	135
Flemensfirth	Space Cadet	7	g	133
Flemensfirth	Stand Up And Fight	5	g	130
Flemensfirth	Strong Pursuit	7	g	139
Flemensfirth	Sumos Novios	9	g	139
Flemensfirth	Sydney Paget	10	g	130
Flemensfirth	The Last Samuri	9	g	161
Flemensfirth	Three Musketeers	7	g	152
Flemensfirth	Two Taffs	7	g	139
Flemensfirth	Viva Steve	9	g	139
Flemensfirth	Waiting Patiently	6	g	151
Fragrant Mix	Bloody Mary	6	m	133
Fragrant Mix	Mixboy	7	g	140
Fragrant Mix	Relax	12	g	131
Galileo	Ballyglasheen	7	g	133
Galileo	Celestial Prospect	10	g	130

Sire	Horse	Age	Sex	Official Rating as of January 2017
Galileo	Iniciar	7	g	130
Galileo	Leo Luna	8	g	131
Galileo	Marchese Marconi	8	g	142
Galileo	Moidore	8	g	130
Galileo	Shelford	8	g	146
Galileo	Supasundae	7	g	146
Galileo	Windsor Park	8	g	153
Germany	Faugheen	9	g	176
Germany	Free Expression	8	g	142
Germany	Germany Calling	8	g	145
Germany	Moon Over Germany	6	g	134
Gold Well	Arctic Gold	6	g	138
Gold Well	Bally Longford	9	g	135
Gold Well	Ballyboker Breeze	9	g	140
Gold Well	Clondaw Cian	7	g	138
Gold Well	Dark Flame	8	g	135
Gold Well	Forever Gold	10	g	131
Gold Well	General Principle	8	g	133
Gold Well	Gold Futures	8	g	147
Gold Well	Holywell	10	g	152
Gold Well	Johns Spirit	10	g	134
Gold Well	Kylecrue	10	g	134
Gold Well	Legacy Gold	9	m	138
Gold Well	Looking Well	8	g	132
Gold Well	Monbeg Gold	7	g	129
Gold Well	Mysteree	9	g	129
Gold Well	Poker School	7	g	132
Gold Well	Saints And Sinners	9	g	130
Gold Well	Sausalito Sunrise	9	g	155
Gold Well	Some Are Lucky	6	g	132
Gold Well	The Unit	6	g	131
Hernando	Clyne	7	g	148
Hernando	Conquisto	12	g	138
Hernando	Desoto County	8	g	137
Hernando	Draco	8	g	136
Hernando	First Fandango	10	g	130
Hernando	Make A Track	11	g	144
Hernando	Sandymount Duke	8	g	142
Hernando	Slowfoot	9	h	135
Heron Island	Bay Of Freedom	8	g	135
Heron Island	Bishops Road	9	g	147
Heron Island	Black Hercules	8	g	156
Heron Island	Blue Heron	9	g	147
Heron Island	Heron Heights	8	g	138
Heron Island	If In Doubt	9	g	153
Heron Island	Inner Drive	9	g	138
Heron Island	Otago Trail	9	g	151
Heron Island	Trustan Times	11	g	132
High Chaparral	Altior	7	g	160
High Chaparral	Caracci Apache	7	g	135

Sire	Horse	Age	Sex	Official Rating as of January 2017
High Chaparral	Different Gravey	7	g	160
High Chaparral	Hadrian's Approach	10	g	140
High Chaparral	Hawk High	7	g	140
High Chaparral	Landofhopeandglory	4	g	137
High Chaparral	Surtee Du Berlais	7	m	139
Kalanisi	Another Hero	8	g	136
Kalanisi	Barters Hill	7	g	146
Kalanisi	Brain Power	6	g	162
Kalanisi	Champagne Express	7	g	130
Kalanisi	Hannah's Princess	8	m	132
Kalanisi	Kalane	8	m	138
Kalanisi	Rainy City	7	g	135
Kalanisi	Templehills	6	g	131
Kapgarde	A Vos Gardes	7	g	130
Kapgarde	Alisier D'Irlande	7	g	144
Kapgarde	As De Mee	7	g	145
Kapgarde	Clan Des Obeaux	5	g	152
Kapgarde	Dolos	4	g	136
Kapgarde	Edgardo Sol	10	g	144
Kapgarde	Fixe Le Kap	5	g	138
Kapgarde	Garde La Victoire	8	g	158
Kapgarde	Hammersly Lake	9	g	142
Kapgarde	Kaki De La Pree	10	g	137
Kapgarde	Ubak	9	g	150
Kapgarde	Ultragold	9	g	139
Karinga Bay	Coneygree	10	g	166
Karinga Bay	Karinga Dancer	11	g	140
Karinga Bay	Killala Quay	10	g	130
Karinga Bay	No Duffer	10	g	144
Kayf Tara	All The Answers	6	g	132
Kayf Tara	Arthur's Oak	9	g	150
Kayf Tara	Ballyandy	6	g	135
Kayf Tara	Ballybolley	8	g	135
Kayf Tara	Blaklion	8	g	152
Kayf Tara	Bold Henry	11	g	140
Kayf Tara	Brother Tedd	8	g	149
Kayf Tara	Bucking The Trend	9	g	132
Kayf Tara	Cantlow	12	g	130
Kayf Tara	Carole's Destrier	9	g	154
Kayf Tara	Carruthers	14	g	140
Kayf Tara	Champagne At Tara	8	g	135
Kayf Tara	Constantine Bay	6	g	136
Kayf Tara	Edwulf	8	g	143
Kayf Tara	Fahamore	10	g	130
Kayf Tara	Final Nudge	8	g	137
Kayf Tara	Flintham	8	g	144
Kayf Tara	Gone Too Far	9	g	131
Kayf Tara	Gully's Edge	7	g	135
Kayf Tara	Identity Thief	7	g	159
Kayf Tara	Javert	8	g	147

Sire	Horse	Age	Sex	Official Rating as of January 2017
Kayf Tara	Just Cameron	10	g	149
Kayf Tara	Kayf Blanco	8	g	136
Kayf Tara	Lieutenant Colonel	8	g	149
Kayf Tara	Lifeboat Mona	7	m	144
Kayf Tara	Long Lunch	8	g	132
Kayf Tara	Mozoltov	11	g	149
Kayf Tara	Mystical Knight	8	g	139
Kayf Tara	No Comment	6	g	137
Kayf Tara	No Planning	10	g	142
Kayf Tara	North Hill Harvey	6	g	147
Kayf Tara	Premier Bond	7	g	137
Kayf Tara	Rathlin	12	g	137
Kayf Tara	Relentless Dreamer	8	g	138
Kayf Tara	Rons Dream	7	m	145
Kayf Tara	Sign Of A Victory	8	g	150
Kayf Tara	Solstice Star	7	g	140
Kayf Tara	Special Tiara	10	g	160
Kayf Tara	Spirit Of Kayf	6	g	135
Kayf Tara	Tapaculo	6	g	133
Kayf Tara	Tara Flow	7	m	131
Kayf Tara	Tara Point	8	m	132
Kayf Tara	Tea For Two	8	g	158
Kayf Tara	The Govaness	8	m	142
Kayf Tara	The Package	14	g	145
Kayf Tara	Thistlecrack	9	g	174
Kayf Tara	Value At Risk	8	g	146
Kayf Tara	War Sound	8	g	148
King's Theatre	Acting Lass	6	g	135
King's Theatre	Baby Shine	11	m	134
King's Theatre	Baily Green	11	g	141
King's Theatre	Ballychorus	8	m	141
King's Theatre	Ballycross	6	g	133
King's Theatre	Band Of Blood	9	g	135
King's Theatre	Bellshill	7	g	150
King's Theatre	Blood Crazed Tiger	6	g	138
King's Theatre	Born Survivor	6	g	143
King's Theatre	Briery Belle	8	m	144
King's Theatre	Briery Queen	8	m	144
King's Theatre	Carlingford Lough	11	g	166
King's Theatre	Carrigmoorna Rock	9	m	133
King's Theatre	Carrigmorna King	11	g	140
King's Theatre	Cogry	8	g	134
King's Theatre	Cue Card	11	g	170
King's Theatre	Diamond King	9	g	155
King's Theatre	Draytonian	7	g	130
King's Theatre	Electric Concorde	6	g	135
King's Theatre	Fethard Player	10	g	150
King's Theatre	Fine Theatre	7	g	134
King's Theatre	Fingal Bay	11	g	141
King's Theatre	For Good Measure	6	g	138

Sire	Horse	Age	Sex	Official Rating as of January 2017
King's Theatre	Fourth Act	8	g	135
King's Theatre	Gusty Rocky	8	g	136
King's Theatre	Happy Diva	6	m	137
King's Theatre	Jacks Last Hope	8	g	133
King's Theatre	Junction Fourteen	8	g	148
King's Theatre	Katie Too	6	m	132
King's Theatre	Killiney Court	8	g	132
King's Theatre	Kings Bandit	9	g	134
King's Theatre	Kings Lad	10	g	135
King's Theatre	King's Odyssey	8	g	145
King's Theatre	Kings Palace	9	g	152
King's Theatre	Kingswell Theatre	8	g	130
King's Theatre	L'Ami Serge	7	g	152
King's Theatre	Lily Waugh	10	m	138
King's Theatre	Lyrical Theatre	8	m	130
King's Theatre	Master Dee	8	g	144
King's Theatre	Mendip Express	11	g	141
King's Theatre	Menorah	12	g	163
King's Theatre	Minella Aris	6	g	130
King's Theatre	Minella Charmer	6	g	139
King's Theatre	Minella Foru	8	g	146
King's Theatre	Minella Reception	11	g	135
King's Theatre	Minellacelebration	7	g	130
King's Theatre	Minellaforleisure	9	g	132
King's Theatre	Monbeg Theatre	8	g	130
King's Theatre	Monkey Kingdom	9	g	135
King's Theatre	Morello Royale	7	m	135
King's Theatre	Morning Royalty	10	g	135
King's Theatre	Morning Run	8	m	145
King's Theatre	Murrayana	7	g	131
King's Theatre	No Secrets	13	g	136
King's Theatre	Peregrine Run	7	g	140
King's Theatre	Perfect Gentleman	12	g	139
King's Theatre	Perform	8	g	134
King's Theatre	Pete The Feat	13	g	132
King's Theatre	Portway Flyer	9	g	131
King's Theatre	Prince Tom	13	g	135
King's Theatre	Regal Encore	9	g	150
King's Theatre	Royal Regatta	9	g	158
King's Theatre	Royal Vacation	7	g	143
King's Theatre	Royale Knight	11	g	136
King's Theatre	Shaneshill	8	g	156
King's Theatre	Shuil Royale	12	g	149
King's Theatre	Solita	8	m	132
King's Theatre	Southfield Theatre	9	g	152
King's Theatre	Stephanie Frances	9	m	138
King's Theatre	Sumkindofking	6	g	132
King's Theatre	Sunshine Corner	6	m	134
King's Theatre	Tagrita	9	m	139
King's Theatre	The Druids Nephew	10	g	146

Sire	Horse	Age	Sex	Official Rating as of January 2017
King's Theatre	The Dutchman	7	g	139
King's Theatre	The Gipper	7	g	130
King's Theatre	The New One	9	g	163
King's Theatre	Theatre Guide	10	g	153
King's Theatre	Theatrical Star	11	g	132
King's Theatre	West Wizard	8	g	130
King's Theatre	William Henry	7	g	132
King's Theatre	Wings Of Smoke	12	g	132
Midnight Legend	Bally Legend	12	g	140
Midnight Legend	Cresswell Breeze	7	m	133
Midnight Legend	Crosspark	7	g	132
Midnight Legend	Dusky Legend	7	m	135
Midnight Legend	Knight Bachelor	7	g	137
Midnight Legend	Meet The Legend	6	g	138
Midnight Legend	Mercian Prince	6	g	135
Midnight Legend	Midnight Jazz	7	m	140
Midnight Legend	Midnight Prayer	12	g	133
Midnight Legend	Midnight Shot	7	g	132
Midnight Legend	Midnight Tour	7	m	133
Midnight Legend	Miss Crick	6	m	136
Midnight Legend	Molly's A Diva	10	m	139
Midnight Legend	Pearls Legend	10	g	135
Midnight Legend	Potters Legend	7	g	139
Midnight Legend	Quite By Chance	8	g	147
Midnight Legend	Seeyouatmidnight	9	g	154
Midnight Legend	Shades Of Midnight	7	g	142
Midnight Legend	Simply A Legend	8	g	135
Midnight Legend	Sir Ivan	7	g	137
Midnight Legend	Sizing John	7	g	153
Midnight Legend	Twelve Roses	9	g	140
Midnight Legend	Warriors Tale	8	g	138
Midnight Legend	Whataknight	8	g	144
Midnight Legend	William H Bonney	6	g	132
Milan	Algernon Pazham	8	g	137
Milan	Anteros	9	g	131
Milan	Apache Stronghold	9	g	153
Milan	Ash Park	9	g	132
Milan	Barrakilla	10	g	136
Milan	Ceasar Milan	9	g	133
Milan	Chalk It Down	8	g	145
Milan	Double Seven	11	g	145
Milan	Double Shuffle	7	g	149
Milan	El Bandit	6	g	139
Milan	Emerging Force	7	g	146
Milan	Falcon Crest	7	g	136
Milan	Fascino Rustico	9	g	130
Milan	Florrie Boy	6	g	133
Milan	Full Cry	7	g	135
Milan	Guess Again	12	g	130
Milan	Gullinbursti	11	g	139

Sire	Horse	Age	Sex	Official Rating as of January 2017
Milan	Isaacstown Lad	10	g	131
Milan	Jessber's Dream	7	m	136
Milan	Jezki	9	g	167
Milan	Join The Clan	8	g	138
Milan	Le Reve	9	g	146
Milan	Lessons In Milan	9	g	140
Milan	Lord Wishes	10	g	133
Milan	Mall Dini	7	g	140
Milan	Man With Van	11	g	133
Milan	Martello Tower	9	g	150
Milan	Max Ward	8	g	134
Milan	Milan Bound	9	g	130
Milan	Milansbar	10	g	144
Milan	Milborough	11	g	135
Milan	Milsean	8	g	145
Milan	Monalee	6	g	139
Milan	Monbeg Notorious	6	g	132
Milan	Mountainous	12	g	133
Milan	Night In Milan	11	g	139
Milan	One For Arthur	8	g	147
Milan	Operating	10	g	138
Milan	Ordinary World	7	g	144
Milan	Rogue Trader	8	g	137
Milan	Rum And Butter	9	g	130
Milan	Singlefarmpayment	7	g	142
Milan	Sizing Granite	9	g	154
Milan	Some Buckle	8	g	134
Milan	Sort It Out	8	g	141
Milan	The Eaglehaslanded	7	g	142
Milan	The Paparrazi Kid	10	g	141
Milan	Tornado In Milan	11	g	135
Milan	Ttebbob	8	g	143
Milan	Two Rockers	10	g	130
Milan	Viens Chercher	6	g	134
Milan	What A Moment	7	g	134
Milan	You Say What	7	g	132
Montjeu	Argocat	9	g	156
Montjeu	Gabrial The Great	8	g	138
Montjeu	Gassin Golf	8	g	133
Montjeu	Hassle	8	g	133
Montjeu	Hurricane Fly	13	g	168
Montjeu	Ivanovich Gorbatov	5	g	150
Montjeu	John Constable	6	g	131
Montjeu	Noble Prince	13	g	135
Montjeu	Open Eagle	8	g	140
Montjeu	Pearl Castle	7	g	137
Montjeu	Plinth	7	g	135
Montjeu	Tigris River	6	g	138
Old Vic	Bally Beaufort	9	g	135
Old Vic	Ballyoptic	7	g	162

Sire	Horse	Age	Sex	Official Rating as of January 2017
Old Vic	Boyfromnowhere	10	g	130
Old Vic	Call Me Vic	10	g	138
Old Vic	Carningli	8	g	133
Old Vic	Colour Squadron	11	g	139
Old Vic	Grand Vision	11	g	137
Old Vic	Gurkha Brave	9	g	135
Old Vic	Join Together	12	g	145
Old Vic	Kie	9	g	133
Old Vic	Killultagh Vic	8	g	153
Old Vic	Knock House	8	g	141
Old Vic	Lamb Or Cod	10	g	138
Old Vic	Land Of Vic	9	m	134
Old Vic	Pendra	9	g	145
Old Vic	Real Steel	9	g	143
Old Vic	Silvergrove	9	g	135
Old Vic	Southfield Vic	8	g	140
Old Vic	Spring Heeled	10	g	141
Old Vic	Toby Lerone	10	g	131
Old Vic	Vics Canvas	14	g	145
Old Vic	Village Vic	10	g	158
Old Vic	Westend Star	8	g	138
Oscar	Apache Jack	9	g	130
Oscar	At Fishers Cross	10	g	146
Oscar	Bags Groove	6	g	134
Oscar	Ballycrystal	6	g	130
Oscar	Be The Hero	6	g	130
Oscar	Buachaill Alainn	10	g	134
Oscar	Cara's Oscar	11	g	136
Oscar	Chill Factor	8	g	138
Oscar	Clean Sheet	8	g	132
Oscar	Clondaw Kaempfer	9	g	135
Oscar	Courtown Oscar	8	g	130
Oscar	Cusheen Bridge	9	g	131
Oscar	Dashing Oscar	7	g	132
Oscar	Days Hotel	12	g	148
Oscar	Draycott Place	8	g	137
Oscar	Dressedtothenines	10	m	138
Oscar	Drumacoo	8	g	143
Oscar	Felix Yonger	11	g	162
Oscar	Finian's Oscar	5	g	149
Oscar	Gallant Oscar	11	g	146
Oscar	God's Own	9	g	165
Oscar	Jetson	12	g	149
Oscar	Kashline	11	g	135
Oscar	Lake View Lad	7	g	135
Oscar	Local Show	9	g	141
Oscar	Lord Windermere	11	g	152
Oscar	Mallowney	11	g	157
Oscar	Montys Meadow	9	g	140
Oscar	Never Enough Time	9	g	130

Sire	Horse	Age	Sex	Official Rating as of January 2017
Oscar	No No Mac	8	g	130
Oscar	O Maonlai	9	g	143
Oscar	Oathkeeper	7	g	132
Oscar	O'Faolains Boy	10	g	151
Oscar	Off The Ground	11	g	132
Oscar	One For The Guv'Nr	8	g	131
Oscar	Onenightinvienna	8	g	146
Oscar	Oscar Knight	8	g	135
Oscar	Oscar Rock	9	g	147
Oscar	Oscar Sam	8	g	131
Oscar	Oscar Sunset	10	g	134
Oscar	Oscara Dara	12	g	147
Oscar	Oscarteea	8	g	130
Oscar	Our Kaempfer	8	g	148
Oscar	Ozzie The Oscar	6	g	135
Oscar	Pobbles Bay	7	g	145
Oscar	Rather Be	6	g	134
Oscar	Ravished	9	g	135
Oscar	Red Devil Boys	10	g	137
Oscar	Rightdownthemiddle	9	g	133
Oscar	River Wylde	6	g	135
Oscar	Rock On Oscar	7	g	135
Oscar	Rock On Ruby	12	g	160
Oscar	Rocklander	8	g	137
Oscar	Rolling Maul	9	g	135
Oscar	Splash Of Ginge	9	g	139
Oscar	The Tullow Tank	9	g	153
Oscar	Wilde Blue Yonder	8	g	136
Oscar	Working Title	15	g	149
Oscar	Wrath Of Titans	8	g	136
Oscar	Zulu Oscar	8	g	132
Poliglote	Casse Tete	5	g	134
Poliglote	Don Poli	8	g	161
Poliglote	Far West	8	g	150
Poliglote	Let's Dance	5	m	142
Poliglote	Pistol Park	6	g	132
Poliglote	Polisky	10	g	130
Poliglote	Politologue	6	g	152
Poliglote	Roi Des Francs	8	g	157
Poliglote	Top Notch	6	g	157
Poliglote	Wonderful Charm	9	g	154
Presenting	A Good Skin	8	g	134
Presenting	Ballycasey	10	g	162
Presenting	Ballykan	7	g	140
Presenting	Ballymalin	7	g	139
Presenting	Bear's Affair	11	g	142
Presenting	Blakemount	9	g	140
Presenting	Bright New Dawn	10	g	146
Presenting	Call The Cops	8	g	145
Presenting	Centasia	10	m	131

Sire	Horse	Age	Sex	Official Rating as of January 2017
Presenting	Childrens List	7	g	135
Presenting	Competitive Edge	10	g	135
Presenting	Cup Final	8	g	146
Presenting	Daisy's Gift	10	m	133
Presenting	Doctor Harper	9	g	143
Presenting	Doing Fine	9	g	130
Presenting	Dromnea	10	g	132
Presenting	Duke Of Navan	9	g	146
Presenting	Dunraven Storm	12	g	144
Presenting	Exxaro	7	g	130
Presenting	First Lieutenant	12	g	139
Presenting	Gold Present	7	g	137
Presenting	Goodtoknow	9	g	137
Presenting	Goonyella	10	g	147
Presenting	Haymount	8	g	144
Presenting	Home Farm	10	g	142
Presenting	Horatio Hornblower	9	g	132
Presenting	Imperial Presence	6	g	130
Presenting	Leave At Dawn	7	g	137
Presenting	Lord Scoundrel	8	g	156
Presenting	Marinero	8	g	140
Presenting	Minella Present	8	g	137
Presenting	More Buck's	7	g	134
Presenting	Mount Mews	6	g	133
Presenting	Movewiththetimes	6	g	136
Presenting	Mr Diablo	8	g	133
Presenting	My Murphy	11	g	148
Presenting	Myska	7	m	136
Presenting	No More Heroes	8	g	159
Presenting	On His Own	13	g	142
Presenting	Pair Of Jacks	9	g	135
Presenting	Peoples Park	8	g	130
Presenting	Pleasant Company	9	g	148
Presenting	Port Melon	9	g	136
Presenting	Present Man	7	g	142
Presenting	Present View	9	g	140
Presenting	Presenting Arms	10	g	145
Presenting	Rogue Angel	9	g	141
Presenting	Saddlers Encore	8	g	132
Presenting	Sedgemoor Express	9	g	130
Presenting	Sizing Coal	9	g	133
Presenting	Snow Falcon	7	g	157
Presenting	Soll	12	g	149
Presenting	Southfield Royale	7	g	147
Presenting	Stellar Notion	9	g	139
Presenting	Sugar Baron	7	g	135
Presenting	Sunni May	6	g	140
Presenting	Templeross	6	g	130
Presenting	Theo's Charm	7	g	135
Presenting	Three Wise Men	7	g	135

Sire	Horse	Age	Sex	Official Rating as of January 2017
Presenting	Thunder And Roses	9	g	141
Presenting	Top Gamble	9	g	159
Presenting	Up For Review	8	g	148
Presenting	Vintage Star	11	g	140
Presenting	Warden Hill	9	g	136
Presenting	Yorkhill	7	g	154
Robin Des Champs	Au Quart De Tour	7	g	136
Robin Des Champs	Champers On Ice	7	g	146
Robin Des Champs	Churchtown Champ	7	g	142
Robin Des Champs	Duke Des Champs	7	g	139
Robin Des Champs	Fire In Soul	6	g	135
Robin Des Champs	Geordie Des Champs	6	g	135
Robin Des Champs	Hell's Kitchen	6	g	139
Robin Des Champs	Listen Dear	7	m	140
Robin Des Champs	Quinz	13	g	139
Robin Des Champs	Robinshill	6	g	141
Robin Des Champs	Si C'Etait Vrai	11	g	137
Robin Des Champs	Simon Squirrel	7	g	134
Robin Des Champs	Sir Des Champs	11	g	150
Robin Des Champs	Sizing Tennessee	9	g	140
Robin Des Champs	Stone Hard	7	g	139
Robin Des Champs	Tombstone	7	g	147
Robin Des Champs	Tour Des Champs	10	g	142
Robin Des Champs	Un Temps Pour Tout	8	g	156
Robin Des Champs	Urban Hymn	9	g	135
Robin Des Champs	Vautour	8	g	176
Robin Des Champs	Vieux Lille	7	g	137
Robin Des Champs	Welsh Shadow	7	g	140
Robin Des Champs	Woodland Opera	7	g	140
Saddler Maker	Alpha Des Obeaux	7	g	155
Saddler Maker	Apple's Jade	5	m	153
Saddler Maker	Bouvreuil	6	g	145
Saddler Maker	Bristol De Mai	6	g	166
Saddler Maker	Cepage	5	g	132
Saddler Maker	Label Des Obeaux	6	g	137
Saddler Maker	Messire Des Obeaux	5	g	143
Saint Des Saints	Aux Ptits Soins	7	g	152
Saint Des Saints	Balbir Du Mathan	8	g	137
Saint Des Saints	Connetable	5	g	144
Saint Des Saints	Dauphine Ereine	5	m	130
Saint Des Saints	Days Of Heaven	7	g	136
Saint Des Saints	Djakadam	8	g	168
Saint Des Saints	Dolores Delightful	7	m	133
Saint Des Saints	Irish Saint	8	g	148
Saint Des Saints	Le Rocher	7	g	138
Saint Des Saints	Lyreen Legend	10	g	145
Saint Des Saints	Romain De Senam	5	g	139
Saint Des Saints	Saint Lino	6	g	132
Saint Des Saints	Sainte Ladylime	6	m	130
Saint Des Saints	Sambremont	7	g	136

Sire	Horse	Age	Sex	Official Rating as of January 2017
Saint Des Saints	Sametegal	8	g	149
Saint Des Saints	The Saint James	6	g	144
Saint Des Saints	Wait For Me	7	g	138
Shantou	Airlie Beach	7	m	141
Shantou	All Hell Let Loose	8	g	136
Shantou	Ballagh	8	g	131
Shantou	Ballynagour	11	g	158
Shantou	Battle Of Shiloh	8	g	142
Shantou	Beware The Bear	7	g	145
Shantou	Briar Hill	9	g	142
Shantou	Bun Doran	6	g	140
Shantou	Carriganog	8	g	134
Shantou	Death Duty	6	g	148
Shantou	Deep Trouble	10	g	133
Shantou	Exactoris	6	g	130
Shantou	Heath Hunter	10	g	130
Shantou	Herbert Park	7	g	134
Shantou	Jimmy Two Times	8	g	135
Shantou	Measureofmydreams	9	g	146
Shantou	Morning Assembly	10	g	149
Shantou	Mr Shantu	8	g	132
Shantou	Polly Peachum	9	m	146
Shantou	Shantou Bob	9	g	146
Shantou	Shantou Flyer	7	g	156
Shantou	Shantou Magic	10	g	130
Shantou	Shantou Village	7	g	146
Shantou	Super Duty	11	g	132
Shantou	Taj Badalandabad	7	g	138
Shantou	The Tourard Man	11	g	140
Shantou	Tully East	7	g	138
Shantou	Wounded Warrior	8	g	152
Shirocco	Annie Power	9	m	166
Shirocco	Art Of Payroll	8	g	134
Shirocco	Lac Fontana	8	g	139
Shirocco	Mijhaar	9	g	134
Shirocco	Minella Rocco	7	g	158
Shirocco	Rock The Kasbah	7	g	150
Sinndar	De Vous A Moi	9	g	132
Sinndar	Hargam	6	g	146
Sinndar	Noble Inn	7	g	133
Sir Harry Lewis	Fourovakind	12	g	130
Sir Harry Lewis	Harry's Farewell	10	g	132
Sir Harry Lewis	Loose Chips	11	g	139
Sir Harry Lewis	Restless Harry	13	g	141
Sir Harry Lewis	Thomas Brown	8	g	142
Sir Harry Lewis	Unowhatimeanharry	9	g	167
Stowaway	Anchor Man	5	g	134
Stowaway	Ballydine	7	g	139
Stowaway	Champagne Fever	10	g	157
Stowaway	Fire In His Eyes	6	g	131

Sire	Horse	Age	Sex	*Official Rating* as of January 2017
Stowaway	Hidden Cyclone	12	g	154
Stowaway	Kilcooley	8	g	161
Stowaway	On Fiddlers Green	7	g	130
Stowaway	Outlander	9	g	164
Stowaway	Runfordave	5	g	137
Stowaway	Soupy Soups	6	g	130
Stowaway	Stowaway Magic	6	g	130
Stowaway	The Worlds End	6	g	131
Turgeon	Aerial	11	g	135
Turgeon	Alcala	7	g	130
Turgeon	Anay Turge	12	g	139
Turgeon	Chapoturgeon	13	g	138
Turgeon	La Vaticane	8	m	143
Turgeon	Ma Filleule	9	m	147
Turgeon	Morito Du Berlais	8	g	140
Turgeon	Turcagua	7	g	140
Turtle Island	April Dusk	8	g	133
Turtle Island	Gorsky Island	9	g	133
Turtle Island	Our Island	12	g	130
Turtle Island	Pilgrims Bay	7	g	131
Turtle Island	Seabass	14	g	136
Turtle Island	Shoreacres	14	g	139
Turtle Island	Tinker Time	9	g	130
Turtle Island	Warrantor	8	g	135
Voix Du Nord	Aristo Du Plessis	7	g	135
Voix Du Nord	Bachasson	6	g	146
Voix Du Nord	Bidourey	6	g	135
Voix Du Nord	Defi Du Seuil	4	g	155
Voix Du Nord	Taquin Du Seuil	10	g	161
Voix Du Nord	Un Ace	9	g	138
Voix Du Nord	Unique De Cotte	9	g	140
Voix Du Nord	Val De Ferbet	8	g	136
Voix Du Nord	Vaniteux	8	g	154
Voix Du Nord	Vibrato Valtat	8	g	152
Voix Du Nord	Voix D'Eau	7	g	146
Voix Du Nord	Voix Du Reve	5	g	144
Voix Du Nord	Vroum Vroum Mag	8	m	155
Westerner	Azorian	9	g	138
Westerner	Ballyculla	10	g	133
Westerner	Belmount	8	g	130
Westerner	Billy No Name	9	g	136
Westerner	Boondooma	10	g	152
Westerner	Caid Du Berlais	8	g	146
Westerner	Champagne West	9	g	166
Westerner	Chelsea Flyer	6	g	130
Westerner	Cole Harden	8	g	152
Westerner	Creepy	9	g	130
Westerner	Deputy Dan	9	g	151
Westerner	Eamon An Cnoic	6	g	130
Westerner	Empire Of Dirt	10	g	160

Sire	Horse	Age	Sex	Official Rating as of January 2017
Westerner	Gilgamboa	9	g	159
Westerner	Kansas City Chief	8	g	130
Westerner	Keeper Hill	6	g	138
Westerner	Kilfinichen Bay	9	g	138
Westerner	Lough Derg Spirit	5	g	134
Westerner	Report To Base	5	g	135
Westerner	Solar Impulse	7	g	140
Westerner	Solomn Grundy	7	g	135
Westerner	Stilletto	8	g	141
Westerner	Streets Of Promise	8	m	137
Westerner	Three Stars	7	g	145
Westerner	Total Recall	8	g	130
Westerner	Velocity Boy	8	g	136
Westerner	Vive La France	8	g	130
Westerner	Wade Harper	7	g	130
Westerner	Wakanda	8	g	150
Westerner	West Approach	7	g	149
Westerner	Western Cape	6	g	133
Westerner	Westerner Lady	7	m	140
Westerner	Westren Warrior	8	g	135
Westerner	What A Warrior	10	g	134
Westerner	Wild West Wind	8	g	135
Westerner	Work In Progress	7	g	132
Winged Love	Amore Alato	8	g	137
Winged Love	Baywing	8	g	135
Winged Love	Bless The Wings	12	g	138
Winged Love	Firebird Flyer	10	g	140
Winged Love	Fletchers Flyer	9	g	144
Winged Love	Hunt Ball	12	g	152
Winged Love	Joey Sasa	8	g	139
Winged Love	Josses Hill	9	g	158
Winged Love	Knight Of Noir	8	g	141
Winged Love	Perfect Candidate	10	g	150
Winged Love	Rock Gone	9	g	135
Winged Love	Simply Wings	13	g	130
Winged Love	Some Plan	9	g	148
Winged Love	Spookydooky	9	g	137
Winged Love	Universal Soldier	12	g	142

Published by James Iddiols